Worship in Song

by Jimmy Jividen

Preface by Howard Norton

Printed in the United States of America.

All biblical quotations from the *New American Standard Version*. The author has followed
this version in placing Old Testament quotations in the New Testament text in capital letters.
Some passages have been placed in bold type for emphasis.

Library of Congress Card Number 87-90741

Star Bible Publications, Inc.
ISBN 0-940999-242

DEDICATION

to songleaders

*Who lead others in offering the fruit of lips as a sacrifice of praise to God.

*Who understand that singing is to teach and encourage one another in the assembly.

*Who model and encourage the elements of inner spirit, genuine heart-felt devotion, intelligent understanding and a Divinely authorized pattern for worship in song.

*Who by prayerful forethought about the purpose and needs of the assembly, select songs which allow individual worshippers to fully express their deep personal feelings of devotion, praise and communion.

*Whose leadership brings harmony out of diversity.

*Who understand their grace gift as a stewardship and use it in serving the whole church.

*Who pour themselves out as a drink offering upon the altar of sacrifice and service to others.

ACKNOWLEDGEMENTS

I acknowledge my debt to many people for the material presented in this book. Many of the authors who have influenced my thinking are in the endnotes. Several have shared their research and offered suggestions.

A number have read all or portions of the manuscript and offered valuable suggestions. Among them are Edward Meyers, John McKeel, Kregg Hood, Lynn McMillon, Steve Jividen, Alvin Jennings, Howard Norton and Everett Ferguson. Four song leaders, Tom Chapin, Bob Connel, Gene Bohannan and Paul Dennis, read the material and gave important practical and technical help.

Phil and Boots Nichols, Clark Potts and my wife Shirley have been, from the very first, a constant help in bringing the manuscript into its final form. With great appreciation I acknowledge my debt to them for their help.

TABLE OF CONTENTS

SECTION IV — **THE REAL ISSUES**

SECTION V — **PRACTICAL EXHORTATION**

FOREWORD

As a youngster growing up in the 1940s and 1950s at the Rosen Heights Church of Christ in Fort Worth, Texas, I often heard powerful pulpit preaching about the importance of having *a cappella* music — and *a cappella* music only — in the public worship services of the church. J. Willard Morrow, my beloved uncle and the pulpit minister of that congregation, believed strongly that instrumental music in public church worship was unbiblical and anti-scriptural. A graduate himself of Texas Christian University in the class of 1934 with a major in Bible, he had seen at close range what happened to people in the Restoration Movement when they accepted the principle that it was all correct to add to worship anything that was not expressly forbidden by the Scriptures. When he originally entered TCU in 1926, it had been only 20 years since the 1906 U. S. Census that first listed churches of Christ and Christian Churches as two separate religious groups. The division had occurred between these two groups over the question of how the Bible authorizes, especially in matters relating to the church's organization and worship. No wonder, then, that the Rosen Heights pulpit often addresed the question of the kind of music that churches of Christ should use in the worship to God.

Much has changed in churches of Christ since my early days in Forth Worth. Today, relatively few ministers publicly address the question of church music in their preaching. In fact, for the last 20 or 30 years, we have said little about this issue. As a result, we have thousands of people, young and old, who worship regularly without instrumental music and have no idea why they do. No one bothers to explain to new converts or to young people coming into adulthood that our use of *a cappella* music is a matter of conviction, not necessarily of taste.

Why have so many of our preachers ceased to speak about this issue? There are probably a variety of reasons for the silences, and a person would have to ask each quiet minister his particular motive for not addressing the music question. Some ministers do not speak to the issue because they believe that there is nothing wrong with the use of instrumental music in worship. They do not preach on the subject because to do so would violate their own conscience. They cannot honestly say anything against the use of instrumental music when in their heart of hearts they believe that the insistence on *a cappella* music is much ado about nothing. While I believe that those preachers who feel this way are a minority, I also believe their numbers are greater than most elderships realize.

Rather than state clearly how they feel on the subject, they choose to remain silent and protect their positions and salaries. Others are brave enough to risk their security by stating what they believe on this question, but remain silent in order not to create division in the churches where they preach. Regardless of the motivation behind the silence, these preachers who privately approve the use of instrumental music do not address the subject from their pulpits.

Another group of ministers remain silent because they believe that truth conquered in 1906, and instruments were effectively excluded from churches of Christ, so why continue to talk about the subject. They compare our results over the last 80 years or so and see that the *a cappella* churches of Christ have done exceedingly well in comparison with the Disciples of Christ and the Conservative or Independent Christian Churches. We have produced great scholars, built outstanding educational institutions, grown numerous large congregations, given generously to relieve human suffering at home and abroad, done creditable mission work in various parts of the world, and have seen our own people ascend to key positions in such fields as medicine, law, business, education and politics. With success like this under our belt, some preachers reason, we have conclusively shown that we were right in 1906. We have put the problem to rest and have advanced the cause of Christ. Since we have done so well, they think, we do not need to re-hash old issues like instrumental music. We just need to push ahead. When this kind of mentality exists, there is silence even in the pulpits of the convinced.

Still another group of church leaders who are convinced that *a cappella* music is the only kind of musical praise authorized by Christ for his church believe that the whole issue is irrelevant in today's society. When mankind is facing issues like nuclear war, AIDS, drug addiction, crime, divorce, broken homes, child abuse, famine, abortion, homosexuality, teen-age suicide, runaways, Communism, *apartheid,* and an endless list of other social and moral problems, these leaders reason that an issue like instrumental music in public worship is entirely too insignificant to worry about. Although these well-intentioned, but unwise, brethren are totally committed to *a cappella* music as the only musical form authorized by Christ for his church, they are silent about it because they don't see the need to spend the necessary time or energy to teach about such a "trivial" issue.

Others who occupy our pulpits remain silent because they have not discovered the way to speak effectively to this issue. 1906 was a long time ago. The arguments pro and con have faded in our individual and collective memory. Most of the leaders on both sides of the issue have long since departed, and many in our generation simply do not know how to address the subject. Although I have had ample opportunity to study the music question both with instrumental and a cappella brethren, an experience within the last two or three years reminded me of how little I knew as compared to what a group of older brothers know on the music question. I was privileged to be a part of a discussion in which four Bible scholars, older than I, grappled with the music question. What a rare experience to be in the presence of James O. Baird and the late and beloved Raymond Kelcy of Oklahoma Christian College, Waymon Miller from an *a cappella* church of Christ in Tulsa, and Seth Wilson from Ozark Christian College in Joplin, Missouri. These men, by virture of their years, were not as far removed from the original controversy as I was and am. Their historical perspective contributed greatly to my own understanding of the music question. This book will do the same thing for anyone who takes the time to study it.

Jimmy Jividen, a devout preacher-scholar, believes that the instrumental music issue is relevant at the end of the twentieth century as it was at its beginning. He believes that our preachers and elders must not remain silent any longer on the music question because there is at the very heart of this issue the central question of how we are to interpret and apply the Scriptures. Jividen says,

> It was how the silence of the Scriptures was to be interpreted that was the underlying reason for the division of the Restoration Movement in 1906. Nowhere was the importance of how one regarded the silence of the Scriptures more pronounced than in the use or non-use of instrumental music.
>
> If the silence of the Scriptures on instrumental music means nothing, then its use in Christian worship would not be wrong. One could use it because it was not condemned. The silence of the Scripture would allow men to do what they pleased. Accepting this hermeneutical principle would place a person in the historical stream of the Disciples of Christ and the Conservative Christian Church.
>
> It should be noted that the historical division which exists in the Restoration Movement in the United States involved more than merely the use and non-use of instrumental music. It involved a basic understanding of 'how' the Scriptures teach. . . . The use of instrumental music is just one of the many fruits of accepting a certain hemeneutical principle.
>
> If the 'silence of the Scriptures' is prohibitive, then the use of instrumental music in Christian worship would be wrong. One could not use it because it was not authorized. The silence of the Scriptures would prohibit men from doing what they pleased in worshipping God. Accepting this hermeneutical principle would place one in the historical stream of the churches of Christ.

This book, then, becomes compulsory reading for every person who holds a position on the music question whether that position is instrument or *a cappella*. Jividen has done us a great service by reviewing and evaluating the key arguments for and against instrumental music from the distant past as well as from more recent times.

The very fact that Jimmy Jividen has brought this book into existence places a great responsibility upon every preacher, every elder, and every Christian to restudy carefully the music question. This excellent volume is a resource that we must not neglect.

Preachers and elders, especially, should read the book and address the instrumental issue both publicly and privately. Church leaders do not have to make church music the subject of every sermon nor must they lead with this question in doing evangelistic work. They should, however, make sure that at regular intervals in the life of their congregations the members hear with clarity the reasons why churches of Christ should refuse, as a matter of biblical conviction, to introduce instrumental music into the public worship.

Jimmy Jividen's conclusions are not always predictable. Some readers will be surprised by what he says concerning the use of solos, quartets, and choruses. Some will no doubt wince at what he says concerning the use of instrumental music to accompany religious songs outside the church's public worship. Certain brethren will resent his views on brotherhood and fellowship while others will thank God for what they perceive as insight and courage.

Jimmy Jividen will neither be surprised nor offended by those who question his conclusions. He is an able scholar who is dedicated to the biblical text and is willing to listen to, as well as teach, those with whom he disagrees. He is at once a man of conviction and tolerance. It is a privilege to claim him as a friend and brother.

Howard W. Norton

Editor, Christian Chronicle
Bible Department Chairman, Oklahoma Christian College
July 23, 1987

INTRODUCTION

There is an abundance of material about worshipping God in song in the writings of the Restoration Movement. No issue has been discussed more. No issue has been connected with more emotional feeling between brethren. No issue has caused more division.

Most of the discussion has centered around whether or not to use instrumental music in worshipping God in song. Most of the material has been polemic. Some of the material seems to be in the interest of promoting or justifying parties rather than understanding what is the will of the Lord.

It is hoped that the material in this book will be able to build on the discussions which have gone before and at the same time avoid some of the pitfalls.

Currently there is dialogue between the advocates and the rejectors of instrumental music from among those who have an historical heritage in the Restoration Movement. This dialogue calls for a re-evaluation of the nature and scope of praising God in song.

The discussion of this topic is difficult for many reasons.

It deals with presuppositions. The religious practices of a group are generally determined by the presuppositions which they hold. If there is a difference between them and another group, it sometimes involves culture, traditions, identity with a party or even experiential personal preferences. When brethren begin to think and reason about these differences, however, it ultimately goes back to the presuppositions they hold about authority.

It deals with parties. These parties have historically been identified with and supported by religious papers and Bible colleges. Those in the party form a close identity with their leaders and too often let their leaders do the thinking for them.

It deals with prejudice. When one becomes identified with a party or publicly affirms a position, it becomes difficult for him to change his thinking. He is emotionally involved. It becomes difficult for him to listen to what others are saying if it challenges his position. His mind is made up, and he does not want to be "confused with the facts".

The purpose of the first two sections of this book is to get behind the controversy surrounding instrumental music in the last century and discover the practice and purpose of singing in the New Testatment church. Section three deals with the historical arguments which have been made for and against the use of instrumental music in worship. Section four deals with the basic issues which need to be addressed in resolving the question. Section five deals with practical exhortations to a broken brotherhood in order that there may be "unity of the faith".

UNDERSTANDING TERMS

Any discussion should begin with the definition of terms. Especially is this true if there is disagreement. The meaning that one side gives to a term may be completely different from the meaning the other side gives to it. If the terms are clearly defined, then much of the disagreement may be resolved. Even if the disagreement is not resolved, the different sides will better understand one another.

The discussion of worship in song has particularly been plagued with confusion about the meaning of terms. Terms and concepts have not been understood in the same way by those involved in the discussion.

This section is devoted to two things. First, it clearly defines terms in the New Testament which are connected with worship in song. Second, it gives the theological basis of these terms.

CHAPTER 1

DEFINITIONS

Words for Worship

There are ten Greek terms used for "worship" in the New Testament.[1] Each one conveys a meaning which helps one to understand what is involved in the concept of worship.

Three of these terms, *leitourgeo, latreuo* and *proskuneo*, are used in the context of Christian worship specifically and need to be examined. There is no instance in the New Testament that any of these terms for "worship" apply specifically to singing, praying or observing the Lord's Supper. There are times in which these words might involve specific acts like giving, preaching or teaching.[2] Generally, however, these terms involve worship in a general way rather than in specific acts.

Proskuneo is the word that is most often translated "worship" in the New Testament.[3] It is defined thus:

> . . .*used to designate the custom of prostrating oneself before a person and kissing his feet, the hem of his garment, the ground, etc.; the Persians did this in the presence of their deified king, and the Greeks before a divinity or someth. holy; (fall down and) worship, do obeisance to, prostrate oneself before, do reverence to, welcome respectfully. . .*[4]

Earlier uses of the term in Greek and Jewish literature could mean "veneration to either God or man". In the New Testament the term is

more specialized. Heinrich Greeven defines it thus:
> *When the NT uses proskuneo, the object is always some
> thing—truly or supposedly—divine.*[5]

This idea is confirmed by Peter's rejection of worship from Cornelius
and the rejection of worship of angels in Revelation.[6] Jesus' reply to
the temptation of the Devil shows that worship involved in the term,
proskuneo belonged only to God.
> *YOU SHALL WORSHIP THE LORD YOUR GOD, AND
> SERVE HIM ONLY.*[7]

The idea of "blowing a kiss to one of higher rank" or "casting oneself
to the ground" is included in the meaning of the term.[8] Worship is
not a dialogue with equals. It involves awe, submission and veneration before one who is recognized as superior. The New Testament
protrays this kind of worship as belonging only to God.

A second word translated "worship" in the New Testament is
latreuo .[9] The meaning of this word changed from the classical to the
koine periods. Originally it meant " to work or serve for reward". It
then came to mean "to render service" with no thought of reward.

Latreuo took on an added dimension in the Septuagint.[10]
H. Strathmann identifies this change.
> *It is not enough to say that latreuein has religious signifi-
> cance. One must say that it has sacral significance.
> Latreuein means more precisely to serve or worship culti-
> cally, especially by sacrifice.*[11]

The word took on a purely religious character in the LXX and continued to be so used in the New Testament. It can be defined thus:
> *..serve, in our lit. only of carrying out of relig. duties,
> esp. of a cultic nature, by human beings:*[12]

In references to Christian worship in the New Testament, *latreuo*
focuses on two things.

First, it involves worship as specific physical acts. Prayer and praise may be offered as a sacrifice of "fruit of lips". Such worship is not dependent upon priests, nor is it limited to physical sacrifices.

> *Through Him then let us continually offer up a sacrifice*
> *of praise to God, that is, the fruit of lips that give thanks*
> *to His name.*[13]

Christian sacrifices involve a broad spectrum of things. "Bearing His reproach", "the fruit of lips" and "doing good and sharing" are all a part of the Christian's divine service.[14] The service (*lateruo*) that one offers to God may even be in the form of such specific acts as "preaching the gospel of His Son".[15] Such constitutes worship just as much as the animal sacrifices which were offered in the temple.

Second, it involves the whole life of the Christian as a sacrifice of service. This service (*lateruo*) may be motivated by the inner feelings of gratitude, reverence and awe because "we have received a kingdom which cannot be shaken". This idea is involved in the following passage:

> *Therefore, since we receive a kingdom which cannot be*
> *shaken, let us show gratitude, by which we may offer to*
> *God an acceptable service with reverence and awe; for*
> *our God is a consuming fire.*[16]

The acts or means through which this service is offered are not suggested. It focuses on the motivation for this service.

Lateruo is used by Paul to express that all of life is a "spiritual service of worship".

> *I urge you therefore, brethren, by the mercies of God, to*
> *present your bodies a living and holy sacrifice, acceptable to*
> *God, which is your spiritual service of worship (latreian).*
> *And do not be conformed to this world, but be transformed by*
> *the renewing of your mind, that you may prove what the will*
> *of God is, that which is good and acceptable and perfect.*[17]

This exhortation is made immediately after a doxology which praises the awesome majesty of God. Man's response to this awesome majesty should be the total sacrifice of his body in service (*latreian*).

Worship that is encompassed in the term, *latreuo* , involves all of life. One's moral and ethical conduct, one's social and economic relationships and one's generosity as well as his prayers and praise are worship to God in this sense.

Romans 12:1-2 does not list all of the specifics of how one is to "offer his body". Many things would be involved. It is clear that the "renewing" of the mind and yielding to "the will of God" are involved.

The figurative and general way in which one is to "present your bodies a living and holy sacrifice acceptable to God" is not to be confused with worship in a more specific sense.[18]

There are times and circumstances in life that one draws near to God in a special sense. The Ethiopian eunuch came to Jerusalem "to worship".[19] Paul told Felix that he "went up to Jerusalem to worship".[20] More was involved in worship in these passages than every day piety. It involved specific acts in specific places at specific times.

There is a general way in which one offers himself as a sacrifice to God in everyday-everyway piety. One also can worship God at specific times, in specific circumstances and with specific acts.

Christian worship is not confined to certain times, like the Sabbath, or certain places, like Jerusalem. It does however, sometimes include special acts at special times and in special places. This is true of the Lord's Supper. It is to be observed at a special time, the first day of the week.[21] It is observed in specific circumstances, with Christians when they meet together.[22] It is to be observed with certain elements and in certain ways. Ignoring such things caused the Corinthians to partake of the Lord's Supper in an "unworthy way" and "to be guilty of the body and the blood of the Lord".[23]

Paul corrected them because they did not see the distinction between observing the Lord's Supper and eating a common meal.[24]

When they assembled, they should have done that which had been commanded by the Lord and exemplified in the early church. They profaned that which was hallowed by the Lord Himself. They could not justify their neglect of observing the Lord's Supper on the basis that " all of life is worship" or that Christian worship does not consist of "special acts on special days and in special circumstances".

Just as one cannot substitute religious ritual for a righteous and moral life, one must not substitute moral goodness for specific acts of worship that God desires from those who serve Him.

The two words that are mainly used with reference to Christian worship are found together in a statement of Jesus. In His response to the Devil Jesus used both terms.

> *YOU SHALL WORSHIP (proskuneseis) THE LORD YOUR GOD, AND SERVE (latreuseis) HIM ONLY.*[25]

The first term emphasizes the sense of awe, submission and veneration to a superior. The second term emphasizes sacrifice and/or service that is given as homage.

A third word that is closely associated with the idea of worship in the New Testament is *leitourgeo*.[26] The English word, "liturgy" is derived from this word. Though generally translated "worship", the idea of "service" or "ministry" is best understood in this term. In the New Testament it always has a religious connotation.[27]

This word is used for the contribution Paul was seeking from Achaia and Macedonia for the brethren in Jerusalem.[28] The same word is used for the contribution which Philippi sent to Paul by Epaphroditus.[29] It is used for Paul's own ministry of preaching the Gospel.[30] Luke uses it with reference to the prophetic and teaching ministry of Paul and others at Antioch.[31]

There is no reference to "singing", "praying" and the "Lord's Supper" being connected with the three words, *leitourgeo, latreuo, proskuneo* , which are associated with worship in the New Testament.[32] This does not mean that singing and praying are not worship. The context in which these special expressions of devotion and praise are found shows them to be worship directed to God.

This absence does not indicate that there are no special "acts of worship". Certain "acts of worship" are to be given at certain times and in certain circumstances which are distinct from a general piety that the Christian expresses in all of life. One who is suffering is to pray. One who is merry is to sing.[33] This is distinct from and more than the service (*latreuo*) which involves all of life, all of the time, in all places and all circumstances.

It is just as unbiblical for one to deny that special acts at special times done in special ways are worship to God as it is to deny that, in another sense, all of life's activities are a sacrifice to God as worship. The correct response to those who see worship as only taking place with certain ritual acts in the assembly is not to deny their validity.[34] One must show that there is a sense in which worship is more than these acts and involves a life of piety. One must also show the external acts, of themselves, are not worship. Worship involves the mind, the spirit and the heart of the worshipper.

In a figurative sense, Paul discribed his life as being "poured out like a drink offering" to God.[35] This did not mean that there were not specific acts of devotion and praise he gave to God within the framework of a total life of sacrifice. Paul told the Corinthians that when they came together on the first day of the week (a specific time) that they were to lay by in store (a specific act) so that there would not need to be gatherings when he came (a specific reason).

Words Associated with Worship

There are a number of words which imply worship from the context in which they are used. They are not translated "worship", nor does Scripture define them as "worship" in a technical sense. They must be considered as part of worship because their very nature implies that they are heart-felt adoration to God.

One such word is "praise".[36] The most common word translated "to praise" is *aineo* .

> *It denotes the joyful praise of God expressed in doxology, hymn or prayer, whether by individuals (Lk. 2:20; Acts 3:8f), the group of disciples (Lk. 19:37), the community (Acts 2:47;*

Rev. 19:5) or the angels (Lk. 2:13).[37]
A form of this word is used to express that Christian praise is a sacrifice to God.

> *Through Him then, let us continually offer up a sacrifice of praise to God, that is, the fruit of lips that give thanks to His name.*[38]

Christian praise is worship. It is a sacrifice of the "fruit of lips" rather than the animals offered in the temple.

A second New Testament word which involves worship is "prayer". The three words that are most commonly translated prayer in the New Testament are *deesis, proseuche* and *enteuxis*. Their meanings are similar.

> *. . . . deesis, proseuche, enteuxis: pr., as Prof. Grimm re marks, is unrestricted as respects its content, while d. is petitionary; moreover pr. is a word of sacred character, being limited to prayer to God, whereas d. may also be used of a request addressed to men . . . . In I Tim. ii:1 to these words is added enteuxis, which expresses confiding access to God; thus, in combination, deesis gives prominence to the expression of personal need, proseuche to the element of devotion, enteuxis to that of child like confidence, by representing prayer as the heart's converse with God.*[39]

"Thanksgivings" (*eucharistias*) is also used in the same text for the worship offered to God. These four words taken together give a broad dimension of prayer and show its importance to worship.

> *. . . I urge that entreaties, and prayers, petitions and thanksgivings, be made on behalf of all men, for kings and all who are in authority, in order that we may lead a tranquil and quiet life in all godliness and dignity.*[40]

Prayer and praise when addressed to God imply worship. They are spoken of as "sacrifices" to God along with doing good, sharing and suffering.[41] They are acts which are involved in worshipping God.

Assembly

If one is to understand New Testament worship, it is necessary to study the purpose and nature of the Christian assembly[42]

The New Testament often speaks of the Christian assemblies. Christians assembled daily in the temple and praised God.[43] They assembled in times of crisis and prayed.[44] They assembled for prayer.[45] They assembled to solve problems.[46] They assembled to observe the Lord's Supper.[47] They assembled to exercise discipline.[48] In these assemblies they worshipped, encouraged one another, re-solved problems and served one another. The earliest non-Biblical testimony to these assemblies is from Pliny.

> *...they were in the habit of meeting on a certain fixed day before it was light, when they sang in alternate verses a hymn to Christ, as to a god, and bound themselves by a solemn oath, not to any wicked deeds, but never to commit any fraud, theft or adultery, never to falsify their word, nor deny a trust when they should be called upon to deliver it up; after which it was their custom to separate, and then reassemble to partake of food — but food of an ordinary and innocent kind. . .[49]*

The Christian assemblies not only involved edification to those who participated[50] but also worship to God.

There is both horizontal encouragement of one another and perpendicular praise to God in the assembly. To affirm the one is not to deny the other. Paul shows the importance of both in discussing the conduct within the Christian assembly in Corinth. Paul speaks of giving thanks to God, worshipping and praising God in singing and prayer.[51] He also admonishes them "Let all things be done for edifi-cation".[52]

Worship is not merely the performance of religious acts, but also involves the motives and attitudes which are behind these acts. If "acts of worship" are done from duty with drudgery, they would not be acceptable. If the same "acts of worship"[53] are done because the worshipper out of a heart of gratitude desires to please God and obey the commands of Jesus, they are acceptable worship. These "acts of worship" must be Divinely sanctioned; they must be the expression of the spirit of man and fulfill the right purposes.

Worship is more than a program of a skilled performer to please an audience or stimulate an emotional response. Worship is not a spectator sport. The worshippers are the actors; God is the audience for praise and the congregation is the audience for edification.

All worship in the New Testament sense is not the same.

Sometimes the term "worship" is used figuratively. All of life is offered as a service of worship. The emphasis is on daily piety.[54]

Sometimes there is the thought of private and personal devotion to God. The worshipper approaches God in praise and prayer, as Jesus did in the Garden or as one prays in his inner room. One's soul is laid out before God in perpendicular worship.[55]

Sometimes there is the thought of communal worship in the assembly of Christians. There is "one anotherness" in such worship.[56] There is singing to one another.[57] There is waiting upon one another to observe the Lord's Supper.[58]

In the assembly worship there are Divinely sanctioned acts to be done at Divinely sanctioned times. The Lord's Supper is to be observed on the first day of the week when Christians come together.[59] The collection of funds takes place when the assembly occurs on the first day of the week.[60]

Words For Singing and Songs

There are three basic words used for "singing" in the New Testament. The following chart shows the places of their use.

Ado	*Psallo*	*Humneo*
Ephesians 5:19	Romans 15:9	Matthew 26:30
Colossians 3:16	I Corinthians 14:15	Mark 14:26
Revelation 5:9	Ephesians 5:19	Acts 16:25
Revelation 14:3	James 5:13	Hebrews 2:12

Revelation 15:3

Although there is some diversity in the origin of these words in the Greek language, no distinction can be found in their use in the New Testament. The noun forms appear together in Ephesians 5:19 and Colossians 3:16 as psalms (*psalmos*), hymns (*humnos*) and songs (*ode*). Even though many attempts have been made to find different meanings for these words in the New Testament, no objective evidence has been brought forth. This led Heinrich Schlier to write:

> *In the NT there is still no precise differentiation between ode, psalmos, and humnos . . .* [61]

In discussing singing (*adein*) Schlier further suggests that there is no distinction between *adein* and *psallein* in Ephesians 5:19.

The origins of the three terms were different. *Adeo* originally meant just "to sing". *Humneo* originally meant "to sing a song of praise". *Psallo*, however, originally meant "to touch" and then "to pluck" and then later "to play a stringed instrument". The meaning "to play a stringed instrument" seems to have held sway throughout a period of time. By the time the LXX was translated, the definition began to change. Gerhard Delling in his study of the word observed:

> *Hence one must take into account a shift of meaning in the LXX in other passages in which the idea of playing is not evident.* [62]

In the same context, Delling further suggests the shift of meaning of the expression "*aidontes kai psallontes* " as found in Ephesians 5:19:

> *The literal sense "by or with the playing of strings, " still found in the LXX, is now employed figuratively. There is nothing to suggest that psalmos and humnos relate to texts of different genres.* [63]

There is no evidence in the New Testament or the writings of the early church that distinction is to be made between psalms, hymns and spiritual songs. There is no evidence that there are differences of usage in *psallo*, *ado* and *humneo* .

ENDNOTES

[1]Four of these terms have the root, *seb* . They are *sebomai* (Mt. 15:19; Mk. 7:7; Acts 16:14; 18:7; 18:13; 19:27), *sebazomai* (Romans 1:25), *sebasma* (II Thess. 2:4) and *eusebeo* (Acts 17:23). The meaning is "to venerate" or in the case of *eusebeo* , "to show piety". Three of the terms are used only one time. Other terms are *doxazo* meaning "to give glory or esteem" (Lk. 14:10), *therapeuo* meaning "to serve, cure or heal" (Acts 17:25) and *threskeia* meaning "religious observances" (Col. 2:18). Three terms, *leitourgeo, latreuo* and *proskuneo*, are used in the context of Christian worship and will be discussed.

[2]See page 5 ff.

[3]It is used at least 59 times.

[4]William F. Arndt and F. Wilbur Gingrich, *A Greek-English Lexicon of the New Testament* (University of Chicago Press, Chicago, 1957), p. 723.

[5]Heinrich Greeven, *"Proskuneo"*, TDNT, Vol. VI, p. 763.

[6]Acts 10:25ff; Revelation 19:10; 22:9.

[7]Matthew 4:10.

[8]Heinrich Greeven, op. cit. p. 759.

[9]It is used 18 times meaning "to serve". (Mt. 4:10; Lk. 1:74; 2:37; 4:8; Acts 7:7; 26:37; 27:23; Rom. 1:9, 25; 12:1; II Tim. 1:3; Heb. 8:5; 9:9,14; 12:28; 13:10; Rev. 7:15; 22:3). It is used 4 times "to worship publicly". (Acts 7:42; 24:14; Phil. 3:3; Heb. 10:2).

[10]LXX will be used in referring to the Septuagint in later references.

[11]H. Strathmann, *"Latreuo "*, TDNT, Vol. IV, p. 60.

[12]William F. Arndt and F. Wilbur Gingrich, op. cit., p. 468.

[13]Hebrews 13:15.

[14]Hebrews 13:13-15.

[15]Romans 1:9.

[16]Hebrews 12:28-29.

[17]Romans 12:1-2.

[18]For a fuller discussion see Hugo McCord, "Worship", *Firm Foundation*, (June 1, 1982), p. 6. In this article he shows that there is more to New Testament worship than merely a holy dedicated life. Worship is also service shown by the term, *latreuo* . This term can mean specific acts at specific times and specific places.

[19]Acts 8:27.

[20]Acts 24:11.

[21]Acts 20:7; I Corinthians 16:1 and 11:20.

[22]I Corinthians 11:20-34.

[23]I Corinthians 11:27.

[24]I Corinthians 11:17-29.

[25]Matthew 4:10.

[26]See Acts 13:2; Rom. 15:16, 27; II Cor. 9:12; Phil. 2:25.

[27]William F. Arndt and F. Wilbur Gingrich, op. cit. pp. 471-472.

[28]Romans 15:27; II Corinthians 9:12.

[29]Philippians 2:25, 30.

[30]Romans 15:16.

[31]Acts 13:2.

[32]Perhaps this was due to the fact that these words had a cultic connotation which made them unsuitable for the new nature of Christian worship. Such words as "praise", "give thanks" and "edify" better denote the idea of Christian worship

[33]James 5:13.

[34]New Testament Christians were involved in special acts in their "worship assemblies". To deny this is to ignore the New Testament evidence. It was "when they came together" (a certain time), they were to observe the Lord's Supper as Paul "received from the Lord" and "delivered" to them (certain acts). See I Corinthians 11:18-34. I Corinthians 12-14 are instructions to the church on what they were to do and not to do in the assembly. Special acts at special times and done in special ways are involved in these instructions. If one defined all of life as worship in every sense, then Paul would not have critizied some at Corinth for speaking in tongues that neither they or others understood.

[35]Philippians 2:17; II Timothy 4:6.

[36]Three words are translated "praise" in the New Testament. *Aineo* is most often used with reference to praising God. *Epaineo* is used in Romans 11:15 from a quotation of Psalms 117:1. *Epaineo* is connection with *doxa* in Philippians 1:11; Ephesians 1:6, 12, 14.

[37]Heindrich Schlier, *"aineo "*, TDNT, Vol. I, p. 177.

[38]Hebrews 13:15.

[39]Joseph Henry Thayer, *A Greek-English Lexicon of the New Testament*, (American Book Company, New York, 1889), p. 126.

[40]II Timothy 2:1-2.

[41]Hebrews 13:13-16.

[42]Ervin Bishop has an important series of articles on "The Christian Assembly" in the *Firm Foundation*, (March 6, 13; June 19, 26; August 7, 14, 1973).

[43]Acts 2:46-47.

[44]Acts 4:23-31.

[45]Acts 12:12.

[46]Acts 15:1-22.

[47]Acts 20:7.

[48]I Corinthians 5:4.

[49]*Letters ,* Book X. xcvi, addressed to Emperor Trajan as quoted by Everett Ferguson, *Early Christians Speak*, (Sweet Publishing Company, Austin, Texas, 1971), p. 81.

[50]Edification, from *oikodomeo ,* means to "encourage, strengthen and build up". It involves people to people encouragement as shown in I Corinthians 14:3, 26 and Hebrews 10:24-25.

[51]I Corinthians 14:14-16, 25.

[52]I Corinthians 14:26.

[53]The phrase, "acts of worship" has had some bad press in recent times. One could just as

well say, "activities of devotion" which would mean the same thing. One could just as well say, "human responses to the numinous" which would convey the same idea. The last phrase might appeal to the theologian. The phrase "activities of devotion" may appeal to the pious monk. The phrase "acts of worship" is probably best understood by the man on the street. It is true that the phrase, "acts of worship", has been stereotyped by reactionary writers in some circles to mean "cold ritual involving mere word worship in the assembly", but such does not nullify the right use of the phrase.

[54]Romans 12:1-2.

[55]Matthew 26:36-46; 6:6.

[56]Everett Ferguson, "New Testament Doctrine of the Christian Assembly, Part III", *Gospel Advocate* (October 17, 1985) shows the nature and purpose of the Christian assembly in the New Testament.

[57]Ephesians 5:19; Colossians 3:16.

[58]I Corinthians 11:33.

[59]Acts 20:7 and I Corinthians 11:17-18.

[60]I Corinthians 16:1-2.

[61]Heinrich Schlier, "*Ado* ", TDNT, Vol. 1, p. 164.

[62]Gerhart Delling, "*Humnos* ", TDNT, Vol. VIII, p. 494.

[63]Ibid., p. 498.

CHAPTER 2

THE NATURE OF WORSHIP IN SONG

Purposes of Worship in Song

To understand fully the New Testament meaning of worshipping God in songs one must focus on what the Scriptures say about its purposes. Three purposes become clear in studying the passages related to singing.

First, there is the purpose of expressing deep feelings. Singing has been called the language of the soul. It expresses, better and more fully than words alone, the deep feelings that are within the heart. It is no accident that singing is to be found in such ceremonies as weddings and funerals. When feelings of joy and sorrow are too deep for mere prose, singing is then used to express the inner feelings of the soul.

After instituting the Lord's Supper in the upper room, Jesus sang a hymn with His disciples.[1] One can hardly imagine greater emotional feelings than were being experienced at that time by both Jesus and His disciples. At such a time, they sang.

When Paul and Silas found themselves in prison, they sang hymns of praise to God.[2] They had been falsely accused, beaten and put in the inner prison with their feet in stocks. Such treatment must have stirred deep feelings. They sang hymns to express these feelings of their heart.

Just as there is singing in sorrow and depression, there is also singing in times of joy. Most individuals know of times in their lives that they would feel like bursting if they could not sing their joy. Such must have been the case of the multitude when Jesus entered Jerusalem on the colt. They "began to praise God joyfully with a loud voice". Luke even preserves what they were saying. It is poetic.

> *BLESSED IS THE KING WHO COMES IN THE NAME OF THE LORD; Peace in heaven and glory in the highest!*[3]

The Pharisees did not think such praise was appropiate and rebuked Jesus. Jesus' response shows that there are times when it seems that only joyful praise can fully express the feelings of the heart.

> *I tell you, if these become silent, the stones will cry out!*[4]

There are a number of poetic passages in the New Testament which some regard as being hymns. Such would be difficult to establish due to the lack of information about their use. These praise passages, which are prominent in Luke, reveal deep personal feelings. The Magnificat, given by Mary on her visit to Elizabeth; the Benedictus, given by Zacharias at the naming of John the Baptist; the praising of the angelic hosts, given at the birth of Jesus; and the praise of Simeon, given upon seeing Jesus in the temple are all poetic and express deep feelings.[5] If they were not originally hymns to sing, they have been made so because they fit the purpose of singing — that of expressing joyful praise.

Singing and praying are means of expressing deep feelings of the soul. When the soul is under stress from sickness and suffering, one can find relief through prayer. When the soul is full of thanksgiving, joy and praise, it can find release in singing. Such is the recommendation of James.

> *Is anyone among you suffering? Let him pray. Is anyone cheerful? Let him sing praises.*[6]

A basic purpose of singing is the expression of inner feelings which come from stress or joy. It fulfills the natural yearning of the soul to find expression. Such is recommended in the Psalms 100.

> *Shout joyfully to the Lord, all the earth.*
> *Serve the Lord with gladness;*
> *Come before Him with joyful singing.*

A second purpose of singing is edification. This purpose was quite distinctive from the worship found in the pagan religions of the first century. Worship of the Greek and Roman idols was performed as civic duty to pacify the anger or to gain the favors of the gods. Worship in the mystery cults was engaged in to gain an experience. Christian worship involved the "one anotherness" of community. What was done in worship to God was also to be done in edification of the church.

> *Teaching and admonishing one another[7]*
> *Pray for one another[8]*
> *When you come together to eat, wait for one another[9]*
> *When you assemble, . . . Let all things be done for*
> *edification[10]*
> *Speaking to one another in psalms, hymns and spiritual*
> *songs[11]*

The importance of understandable and heart felt worship is shown by Paul's admonition to the church at Ephesus:

> *So then do not be foolish, but understand what the will of*
> *the Lord is. And do not get drunk with wine, for that is*
> *dissipation, but be filled with the Spirit, speaking to one*
> *another in psalms and hymns and spiritual songs, singing*
> *and making melody with your heart to the Lord.[12]*

The Dionysus mystery cult was perhaps in the background of this exhortation. Dionysus was the god of wine. Devotees of this cult became drunk in the belief that this allowed the gods to enter them. Their drugged mind would cause them to surrender their will to an experience and act like a drunken fool. In this context, Paul said, "do not be foolish, but understand" and "do not get drunk, but be filled with the Spirit".

Christian worship was to be understandable and rational. The person singing was to do it with the heart, as an expression of inner devotion. The speaking to one another in psalms, hymns and spiritual songs was to be done so it could be understood. Worship involves the expression of inward feelings and is directed upward toward God. Worship also involves those who hear the songs and understand the teaching and are edified.

The edifying purpose of worship in song are shown in Paul's first letter to Corinth. In the context of the abuse of speaking in tongues, Paul showed the importance of both understanding what one says in his worship and also of being understood by others in the assembly.

> *I shall pray with the spirit and I shall pray with the mind also; I shall sing with the spirit and I shall sing with the mind also. Otherwise if you bless in the spirit only, how will the one who fills the place of the ungifted say the "Amen" at the giving of thanks, since he does not know what you are saying?*[13]

It is not clear how the "speaking to one another in psalms. . ." and the "teaching and admonishing one another with psalms . . ." was done.

It could have been solo singing of an individual for the edification of the church. This appears to be what was done in the Corinthian assembly.

> *...When you assemble, each one has a psalm, has a teaching, has a revelation, has a tongue, has an interpretation. Let all things be done for edifying.*[14]

It could have been antiphonal singing in which two groups would sing the lines or phrases of a psalm back and forth to each other.

It could have been responsorial singing in which the congregation would respond in unison to the words of the leader. This appears to be the way Psalms 107 was sung. The leader would sing a story about the plight of Israel being afflicted and in despair. He then would sing how God had responded to their needs. The congregation would respond in unison with the words of the chorus.

> *Let us give thanks to the Lord for His lovingkindness,*
> *and for His wonders to the sons of men!*[15]

Four times this chorus is repeated in the Psalm. It would be the people's response of praise acknowledging God's care and protection.

A third purpose of worship in song is that of praising God. It has already been shown that worship in song is directed "to the Lord". God is the audience. The worshipper is the performer.

Much of what goes on in the name of worship is no more than traditional rituals performed as an ecclesiastical duty and is empty of real devotion to God. Much of what goes on in the name of worship is no more than artistic performances directed to men to stimulate their emotions. The criteria by which it is judged is how the viewers feel rather than if the worship was real. Perhaps no part of worship is more prone to this failing than worshipping in song.

God has always rejected empty "form worship". David recognized that external rituals of sacrifices and burnt offerings were not what God desired. Rather, it was the inward submission of the spirit that God wanted.

> *For Thou dost not delight in sacrifice, otherwise I would*
> *give it; Thou art not pleased with burnt offering. The*
> *sacrifices of God are a broken spirit; A broken and a contrite*
> *heart, O God, Thou wilt not despise.*[16]

God desires worship directed to Him from the heart of man. All of the pomp of men, all of the orderliness of form, all of the beauty of art and all of the emotional stimulation evoked through drama and music cannot substitute for the simple devotion of an humble heart.

In genuine worship, a man pours out his heart, his mind and his spirit as a sacrifice upon the altar of praise. One of the sacrifices which a Christian offers to God is the "sacrifice of praise to God, that is, the fruit of lips".[17]

The three purposes of worship in song are shown in Colossians.

> *Let the word of Christ richly dwell within you; with all wisdom teaching and admonishing one another with psalms and hymns and spiritual songs, singing with thankfulness in your hearts to God.*[18]

Thanksgiving was to come from the heart. Worship was to be directed to God. Teaching and admonishing with psalms, hymns and spiritual songs was to be done to "one another" as well as being addressed to God.

Elements of Worship in Song

The nature of Christian worship can be better understood if one discovers the essential elements which are involved in it.

The Pharisees did not understand these essential elements when they criticized the disciples of Jesus for not washing before they ate bread. They were zealous for the forms handed down by the traditions of the elders, but they had disobeyed the commandments of God by the way they interpreted the Scriptures. Jesus said that they had "invalidated the word of God for the sake of your traditions".[19]

An essential element of worship was that it came from the word of God rather than the traditions of men. Jesus' rebuke to them showed that their worship (*sebontai*) was vain because what they did in the name of worship was without the authority of God. They had set aside the teachings of God in order to practice their own traditions.

> *You hypocrites, rightly did Isaiah prophesy of you, saying,* THIS PEOPLE HONORS ME WITH THEIR LIPS BUT THEIR HEART IS FAR FROM ME. BUT IN VAIN DO THEY WORSHIP ME, TEACHING AS THEIR DOCTRINES THE PRECEPTS OF MEN.[20]

The pages of history are full of examples of God rejecting unauthorized worship. Cain's worship was rejected because it was not offered by faith.[21] Nadab and Abihu displeased God because they offered "strange fire before the Lord, which He had not commanded them".[22] Saul was rejected by God because he presumptuously offered an unauthorized sacrifice. Samuel's statement to Saul showed the importance that God places upon following the will of God in worship.

> *And Samuel said, Has the Lord as much delight in burnt offerings and sacrifices as in obeying the voice of the Lord? Behold, to obey is better than sacrifice, and to heed than the fat of rams.[23]*

Another essential element of Christian worship is that it be in spirit and truth. This is the essential element which was emphasized by Jesus in his conversation with the Samaritan woman.

> *But the hour is coming and now is, when the true worshipper shall worship the Father in spirit and truth; for such people the Father seeks to be His worshippers. God is spirit and those who worship Him must worship in spirit and truth.[24]*

The context of this passage shows that the Samaritan woman was confused about worship. She had asked Jesus if the proper place of worship was in "this mountain" or in "Jerusalem". Jesus' answer was concerned with the inner elements of worship rather than the place of worship. The hour was coming when the place would be unimportant. The important thing would be that God be worshipped in spirit and truth.

To worship "in spirit" means that worship does not necessarily occur in a physical place, like Jerusalem or Mount Gerizim, but in a spiritual realm. God's nature is spirit. Man also has a spiritual nature.[25] The place of communion with God then must be in the spiritual realm. Worship is more than performing physical acts or participating in the right rituals. It is a spiritual communion with God.[26]

To worship "in truth" can mean in the realm of "revealed truth" as found in the Scriptures. If that were the case in this passage, then worship must be in the way that God has instructed. Certainly this understanding would fit with the question the Samaritan woman asked Jesus. She was inquiring about which place was the right place. To worship "in truth" can also mean "genuine" worship as opposed to "pretended" worship.[27] This understanding would also fit the context very well since the Samaritan woman was more concerned with worship being in the right physical place than worship being genuine from the heart or arising from the inner spirit of man.

A third essential element of worship is that it be with the understanding. The physical acts of worship must be authorized by God; the place where worship takes place is in the spiritual realm; it is genuine worship from the heart; it also is that which is understood by the mind.

The importance of "understanding" is shown by Paul in his correcting the abuse of spiritual gifts at Corinth. It would appear that those who possessed the miraculous gift of speaking foreign languages were causing confusion in the assemblies of the church. In their enthusiasm to show off their spiritual gift, they would all speak at the same time in whatever language their gift allowed. Confusion was the result.

Paul tried to correct this situation by showing that one cannot worship God or edify others with words which are not understood. Speaking words in a prayer or a song which one does not understand is not worship. It is unfruitful to the one uttering the words. Speaking words in a prayer or a song which those in the assembly do not understand is not worship. It is confusion.

> *For if I pray in a tongue, my spirit prays, but my mind is*
> *unfruitful. What is the outcome then? I shall pray with the*
> *spirit and I shall pray with the mind also; I shall sing with*
> *the spirit and I shall sing with the mind also. Otherwise if*
> *you bless in the spirit only, how will the one who fills the*
> *place of the ungifted say the "Amen" at your giving thanks,*
> *since he does not know what you are saying?*[28]

The Corinthian Christians in the first century needed to understand what they were saying when they worshipped. So should twentieth century Christians who are tempted to "mouth" the words of their songs and "daydream" during the prayers. The Corinthian Christians of the first century needed to be concerned with edifying others with understandable words in the assembly. Twentieth century Christians should have the same concern when they are tempted to see the assembly as a mere "ritual" performed as a duty to God without edifying the rest of the congregation.[29]

ENDNOTES

[1]Matthew 26:30.
[2]Acts 16:25.
[3]Luke 19:38.
[4]Luke 19:40.
[5]Luke 1:46-55, 68-79; 29-32.
[6]James 5:13.
[7]Colossians 3:16.
[8]James 5:16.
[9]I Corinthians 11:33.
[10]I Corinthians 14:26.
[11]Ephesians 5:19.
[12]Ephesians 5:17-19
[13]I Corinthians 14:15-16.
[14]I Corinthians 14:26.
[15]Psalms 107:8, 15, 21, 31.
[16]Psalms 51:16-17, see also I Samuel 15:22; Micah 6:6-8; Amos 5:22.
[17]Hebrews 13:15.
[18]Colossians 3:16.
[19]Matthew 15:6.
[20]Matthew 15:8-9, see also Isaiah 29:13.
[21]Genesis 4:4; Hebrews 11:4.
[22]Leviticus 10:1.
[23]I Samuel 15:22.
[24]John 4:23-24.
[25]I Corinthians 2:11.
[26]Romans 1:9; Philippians 3:3.
[27]Philippians 1:18 uses "in truth" as the opposite to "in pretense".
[28]I Corinthians 14:14-16.
[29]See pages 9-10 for a discussion of the assembly worship

NEW TESTAMENT PASSAGES

There are thirteen passages in the New Testament which refer to singing.[1] The study of these texts in their context is the first step in drawing any conclusions about the nature, the purpose and the means of worshipping God in song. To draw any conclusions on grounds other than the exegesis of the New Testament texts is to ignore the Scriptures as the source of religious authority. The thirteen passages are listed below with notations as to the way they are used:[2]

OT References	Incidental	Apocalyptic	Basic
Matthew 26:30	Acts 16:25	Revelation 5:9	Ephesians 5:19
Mark 14:26	I Corinthians 14:15,26	Revelation 14:3	Colossians 3:16
Romans 15:9		Revelation 15:3	
Hebrews 2:12	James 5:13		

The context of these passages must be considered to see if they refer to Christian worship or are mere references not directly related to Christian worship in song. A careful study of these passages will show the nature, the purpose and means of singing praise to God.

CHAPTER 3

OLD TESTAMENT REFERENCES

There are four Old Testament references in the New Testament which relate to singing. These must be seen as references to Jewish worship in the Old Testament. Though they are important in seeing the nature of Old Testament worship to God, they neither authorize nor reject any form of Christian worship. These passsages will be seen for what they are in context.

> *Matthew 26:30 — Mark 14:26*
> **And when they had sung a hymn, they went out unto the Mount of Olives.**

The texts of the above passages in Matthew and Mark are identical. They are parallel accounts of Jesus and His apostles singing a hymn at the close of the last Passover Feast that He observed with them. It was during this Passover that the Lord's Supper was instituted by Jesus. After the Supper a hymn was sung before they went out to the Mount of Olives.

Singing was a traditional part of the Passover Feast. Psalms 115-118, which represent the last portion of the *hallel*, were sung in Judaism during the Passover observance as far back as the third century A. D.[3] Such may have been the songs which Jesus sang. Many of the thoughts of these Psalms would have been very appropriate to express the deep feelings which must have been felt by that little group on the night of Jesus' betrayal.

You who fear the Lord, trust in the Lord; He is their help and their shield.

I love the Lord, because He hears my voice and my supplications. Because He has inclined His ear to me, Therefore I shall call upon Him as long as I live. The chords of death encompassed me, and the terrors of Sheol came upon me; I found distress and sorrow. Then I called upon the name of the Lord: O Lord, I beseech Thee, save my life!

Precious in the sight of the Lord is the death of His godly ones.

From my distress I called upon the Lord; The Lord answered me and set me in a large place. The Lord is for me among those who help me; Therefore I shall look with satisfaction on those who hate me.

The stone which the builders rejected has become the chief cornerstone. This is the Lord's doing; It is marvelous in our eyes.[4]

What could be more comforting and reassuring to Jesus when He confronted His betrayal and death than the deep feelings expressed in these Psalms. It was not only the fervent prayers in the garden but also the singing of hymns in the upper room that prepared Jesus for the cross.

If the *hallel* was what was sung by Jesus and the apostles, it would be an example of a psalm (*psalmos*) being hymned (*humneo*). The Gospel writers did not understand that the use of *psallo* and *psalmos* demanded the use of instrumental accompaniment.[5]
Four kinds of worship were practiced by Jews in Jesus' day. Each had certain distinctive elements.

The temple worship at Jerusalem was very elaborate. Richly robed priests with pompous ceremony offered bloody sacrifices with the accompanying elements to appeal to the senses of the worshipper. One could smell the incense along with the burning of animal flesh. This appealed to the sense of smell. There was the flickering of the candles and the ornate trappings of both the temple and the flowing priestly robes. This appealed to the sense of sight. There was the blast of the trumpet, the twanging of stringed instruments and the chant of trained singers. This appealed to the sense of hearing. All in all it was an impressive experience. This type of sense orientated worship was associated with the sacrificial cult. When the temple was destroyed in 70 A. D. animal sacrifices ceased. Along with their ending was the elimination of burning incense, ornate priestly garments, burning of candles and instrumental music. There was no place for such sensory elements outside the temple worship. Eric Werner writes of this temple worship:

> *...Instrumental music, on the other hand, was practiced by the temple's orchestra was invariably understood as an organic accessory of the sacrificial cult. Without sacrifice the instruments had no cultic value.*[6]

The synagogue worship arose during the Babylonian captivity when the temple was in ruin. Circumstances of the captive Jews did not make it possible to practice the priestly ceremonies, animal sacrifices or all that accompanied temple worship. Synagogue worship was more rational than experiential. Inspiration from this worship came through the thought process rather than the sensory stimulation of external ceremonies. The synagogue worship consisted of reading the Scriptures, praying and chanting psalms. It was this type of worship in which Jesus participated in Nazareth.[7] It was this type of worship which most clearly resembles the worship of the New Testament church. Everett Ferguson, after making an extended study of synagogue worship in the first century, makes this summary statement:

> *There remains no evidence that instrumental music was used in synagogue service; indeed this holds true until*

> *comparatively recent times. The real reason for this*
> *absence is probably that advanced by McKinnon, namely*
> *that the instrument was simply irrelevant to the type of*
> *worship developed in the synagogue.*[8]

Family worship was very much a part of the devotion offered by the devout Jew of the first century. The Passover Feast is an example of this type of worship. It was observed in a family type setting.[9] It was a communal meal. It was the remembrance of the exodus. It was a proclamation of hope. This type of worship in the Passover Feast was unlike the experiential worship of the temple. There were no bloody sacrifices, sweet smelling incense or instrumental music. It was also unlike the synagogue worship in that its primary purpose was to teach the family.

This type of worship bound the family together as a unit worshipping God. It looked back to remember the hand of God in the salvation of the nation. It looked forward to the coming of the Messiah. Singing was a part of this family-type of worship. Jesus was doing the traditional thing when He and the apostles hymned a psalm before they left the upper room.

Individual worship is to be found during all of the history of God's people. Abel offered a sacrifice.[10] Abraham privately worshipped God.[11] Many of the Psalms of David are expressions of private devotion. The devout Israelite did not have to wait for the Sabbath to go to the synagogue to pray. He did not have to travel to Jerusalem on a feast day in order to worship Jehovah. Personal piety and private devotion are seen throughout the Old Testament among holy men and women. Daniel prayed three times a day looking toward Jerusalem.[12] Even Gentile "God-fearers" like Cornelius recognized and practiced an "hour of prayer".[13] Private personal devotion was not limited in time and place, nor was it encumbered with devices of sensory show. The sacrifices of an humble and a contrite heart do not need a temple or religious pageantry in order to express itself to God. David expressed this thought in one of his Psalms.

> *For Thou dost not delight in sacrifice, otherwise I would*
> *give it; Thou art not pleased with burnt offering. The*
> *sacrifices of God are a broken spirit; a broken and a*
> *contrite heart, O God, Thou wilt not despise.[14]*

When Jesus, in close fellowship with the apostles, hymned a psalm at
the Last Supper, He was participating in a family type of worship
instituted by Moses to remember the exodus. When Jesus went into
the garden alone, he prayed personally and privately.

The Passover and the ceremonies surrounding it are not a
pattern to follow in Christian worship. It was during the Passover,
however, that the Lord's Supper was instituted by Jesus. The Passover was not to become a part of Christian worship. The Lord's
Supper was to become a part of the Kingdom worship because it was
so authorized by the Lord.[15] This was a new thing and not merely an
extension of the Passover Feast. The fact that Jesus hymned a psalm
after the Passover has no bearing on what hymns are to be sung or
how they are to be sung in the church.

Romans 15:9
**...THEREFORE WILL I GIVE PRAISE UNTO THEE
AMONG THE GENTILES, AND SING UNTO THY
NAME.**

This Old Testament passage is quoted by Paul in affirming God's
acceptance of the Gentiles. The text is found in two Old Testament
passages with almost identical wording.[16] The Psalm was originally
spoken by David when he was delivered from his enemies and is
recorded by Samuel. This Psalm was later included in the book of
Psalms which the Jews used in their praise.

It should be observed that *psallo* is the word translated "to
sing" in this passage and that *humneo* is translated "to sing" in
Matthew 26:30.[17] The New Testament authors seem to use these
words interchangeably when referring to the Old Testament worship
in song.

The context of this passage has nothing to do with Christian worship. Paul is showing in this text how the "fathers" were promised that someday the Gentiles along with the Jews would praise Jehovah. A string of four Old Testament passages are quoted from the Law, the Psalms and the Prophets to validate this point.[18] All these texts point to the time when both Jew and Gentile would be of the "same mind" and with "one accord" and "one mouth" glorify God.[19]

The fathers had been promised that some day this would happen. Paul affirms that such had happened in the church. Both Jew and Gentile with one accord sang praises to God. The passage affirms that unity in Jesus Christ — between Jews and Gentiles — is to be practiced in the church.

Wherefore, accept one another, just as Christ also accepted us to the glory of God.[20]

It is only incidental that singing is mentioned by Paul in this passage. The key thought he wanted to make from the Old Testament Scriptures was that the Gentiles would worship Jehovah along with the Jews. There is nothing in the verse to indicate anything about the nature of Christian worship. The lesson is the unity between Jews and Gentiles.

An analogy might be drawn from the lesson Paul was teaching. God's people in the Old Testament were the Jews. God's people in the New Testament were both Jews and Gentiles who were made one in Christ. Just as there was a change in what constituted the people of God from the Old Testament to the New Testament, there was also a change in what constituted acceptable worship.

Hebrews 2:12
... I WILL DECLARE THY NAME UNTO MY BRETH-REN, IN THE MIDST OF THE CONGREGATION WILL I SING THY PRAISE.

This passage is quoted from Psalm 22:22. It is almost in exact agreement with the LXX.[21] The future tense of *humneo* is the word translated "to sing". This very passage from the Psalms is quoted in the second century document, the Epistle of Barnabas.[22] *Psallo* is the word that is used for "sing" in the Epistle of Barnabas. *Humneo* is the word used by the writer of Hebrews.[23] This would indicate that these words were used interchangeably in New Testament times.

Psalm 22 is a Messianic psalm. It is quoted eleven times in the New Testament referring to Jesus.[24] There are eleven allusions to this Psalm.[25]

The context of this passage is that the author of Hebrews is showing that Christ, the sanctifier, and those who are sanctified are one. It is appropriate that a Messianic psalm be quoted in which the Messiah identifies those in the congregation as "my brethren".

> *For both He who sanctifies and those who are sanctified are all from one Father; for which reason He is not ashamed to call them brethren.[26]*

The quotation from Psalm 22:22 is the first in a string of three Old Testament quotations in the text.[27] The point being made by the author of Hebrews is that Jesus was made "like unto His brethren".[28] The sanctifier and the sanctified are one. Because of this Jesus is able to come to the aid of those who are tempted.

It is only incidental that singing is mentioned in this passage. The author has no intentions of describing Old Testament worship in the temple or giving instructions about the worship of the church.

Conclusion

The three different references to singing in the New Testament which are connected with the worship of the Jews in the Old Testament are of little value in determining what constitutes acceptable worship in the church. Christian worship is different from that of Old Testament Jewish worship in its very nature. Jesus showed this in His conversation with the Samaritan woman.

> *But an hour is coming, and now is, when the true worshipers shall worship the Father in spirit and truth; for such people*

the Father seeks to be His worshipers. God is spirit; and those who worship Him must worship in spirit and truth.[29]

Bloody animal sacrifices, sweet smelling incense and playing instruments fit a period when the ten commandment law was central. But now that Christ and His cross is central, worship forms do not focus on sense perception from observing external rituals. Old Testament worship in the temple was appropiate for its time and its covenant, but it was merely a shadow of things to come. The substance of Christian worship in the New Testament period is of a different nature.

Jesus' observance of the Passover Feast is not a pattern for Christian worship. Incidental references to the singing in the Old Testament quotations do not suggest the nature of worship in song. The study of these passages neither sanctifies nor prohibits anything in Christian worship today.

There are two ways that these passages help in the present study.

First, they show that singing of Psalms was a part of Jewish worship practices from early times and was still being used in the New Testament period.

Second, the way in which New Testament writers and early Christian writers used both *psallo* and *humneo* to refer to singing shows that there was no clear distinction between the words in New Testament times. Their meaning was so similar that they could be interchanged.

ENDNOTES

[1]Besides these references to singing there are a number of passages which are poetic and could well have been early Christian songs. Note: Luke 1:46-55, 68-79; 1:29-32; Philippians 2:6-11; Colossians 1:15-20; Ephesians 2:14-16; 5:14; I Timothy 3:16; II Timothy 2:11-13; I Peter 3:18-22; Revelation 4:11; 5:9-13; 11:15-18; 15:3-4.

[2]OT References refer to Old Testament references in New Testament passages. Incidental refers to passages in which singing in mentioned incidentally. Apocalyptic refers

to passages in which symbolic language is used. Basic refers to passages basic to the nature of New Testament worship in song.

[3]Isidore Singer, *The Jewish Encyclopedia*, Vol. XI (New York: Funk and Wagnall Company, 1905), p. 146.

[4]Psalms 115:11; 116:1-4, 15; 118:4-7, 22-24.

[5]This is contrary to the position taken by Tom Burgess in his book, *Documents on Instrumental Music* (Portland: Scripture Supply House, 1966), p. 117.

[6]Eric Werner, "Musical Aspects of the Dead Sea Scrolls," *The Musical Quarterly*, Vol. 43, No. 1, Janruary, 1957, p. 28.

[7]Luke 4:16

[8]Everett Ferguson, *A Cappella Music in the Public Worship of the Church*, (Abilene, Texas: Biblical Research Press, 1972). p. 36.

[9]Exodus 12:3-4.

[10]Genesis 4:4.

[11]Genesis 12:8.

[12]Daniel 6:10.

[13]Acts 10:30.

[14]Psalms 51:16-17.

[15]Matthew 26:26ff.

[16]II Samuel 22:50; Psalms 18:49.

[17]It is thus translated in the KJV, NASV, RSV, and NIV.

[18]Psalms 18:49; Deuteronomy 32:43; Psalms 117:1; Isaiah 11:10.

[19]Romans 15:5-6.

[20]Romans 15:7.

[21]There is one word variant from the LXX translation of Psalms 21:23.

[22]Epistle of Barnabas VI, 16.

[23]Hebrews 2:12, *"en mesoi ekklesias humneso se"*. and Epistle of Barnabus VI, 16, *"kai psallo anomeson ekklesios agion"*.

[24]Matthew 27:35, 39, 43, 46; Mark 15:24, 29, 34; Luke 23:34, 35-36; John 19:24; Hebrews 2:12.

[25]Matthew 26:24; Mark 9:12; Luke 24:27; John 19:28; Romans 5:5; Philippians 3:2; II Timothy 4:17; I Peter 1:11; Revelation 11:15;19:6.

[26]Hebrews 2:11.

[27]Isaiah 8:17; 8:18.

[28]Hebrews 2:17.

[29]John 4:23-24.

CHAPTER 4

APOCALYPTIC LITERATURE

Three passages in Revelation are considered in this chapter — Revelation 5:9; 14:3; 15:3. They will be considered first as a body of material with similarities in form and content. Then they will be considered individually as a specific text.

There are three things which must be pointed out in considering these passages in Revelation. First, each passage refers to a vision John had of the throne of God around which heavenly beings were giving praise. Second, each consists of apocalyptic literature rich in symbolism. Third, each passage is filled with allusions to Old Testament apocalyptic literature which viewed the Jewish temple worship as the ideal. These three factors must be studied before one can make application of these texts to the life and worship of the church.

The three passages are listed below in their context.

And when He had taken the book the four living creatures and the twenty-four elders fell down before the Lamb, having each one a harp, and golden bowls full of incense, which are the prayers of the saints. And they sang a new song , saying, "Worthy art Thou to take the book, and to break its seals; for Thou wast slain, and didst purchase for God with Thy blood men from every tribe and tongue and people and nation.

And Thou hast made them to be a kingdom and priests to our God, and they will reign upon the earth.[1]

And I looked, and behold, the Lamb was standing on Mount Zion, and with Him one hundred and forty-four thousand, having His name and the name of His Father written on their foreheads. And I heard a voice from heaven, like the sound of many waters and like the sound of loud thunder, and the voice which I heard was like the sound of harpists playing on their harps. And they sang a new song before the throne and before the four living creatures and the elders; and no one could learn the song except the one hundred and forty-four thousand who had been purchased from the earth.[2]

And I saw, as it were, a sea of glass mixed with fire, and those who had come off victorious from the beast and from his image and from the number of his name, standing on the sea of glass, holding harps of God. And they sang the song of Moses the bond-servant of God and the song of the Lamb...[3]

In each of these three passages *ado* is the word translated "to sing" and *ode* is the word translated "song".[4] There is no indication from the text why *ado* is used and *psallo* and *humneo* are not. There does not appear to be any distinction made between *ado, psallo* and *humneo* by the New Testament writers. In both Colossians and Ephesians the verb, *ado* is used with the nouns, *psalmos, humnos,* and *ode* .[5]

    The context of the passages shows that they have no reference to Christian worship. In his vision, John saw the throne of God in future glory. Those around the throne were spiritual beings. To communicate such a vision, he must use human language and associate this language with human experiences which men could understand. Is not this the only way that one can talk about God and His throne? How can one express future reality before it happens? How does one describe spiritual beings participating in spiritual praise? John attempts to do this in symbols with which his readers were familiar — the figurative language of Old Testament apocalyptic literature.

Apocalyptic literature is symbolic. Terms, figures and places are not to be taken literally. Symbols are used to stretch the mind beyond earthly categories of human experiences.

Apocalyptic literature emphasizes that present suffering will be overcome. There is another age coming that will be full of glory. The present reality is nothing to compare with the future ideal.

Many of the symbols used in these passages may have been better understood by the first readers. The identification of the "beast" and his "image" might have been identified with specific men or movements to the readers at the close of the first century. Such is not so clearly understood by those who read nearly 2,000 years later. The identification of the symbols with historical events is not so important as the fact that the passage teaches that the present evil age will be judged and the age to come will bring victory to the right-eous. Each of the three passages in the present study uses symbols in describing the "age to come". It is a mistake to try to make these symbols literal. It is a mistake to impose symbolic references of the "age to come" on the real present situation in the church.

The apocalyptic language of these three passages finds its roots in the apocalyptic literature of the Old Testament. The language of Ezekiel 2:9 lies behind the opening of the sealed book in Revelation 5. The language of Isaiah 42:10 speaks of singing to the Lord "a new song" in a similar fashion that the three passages refer to a "new song". The language of Daniel 7:9-10 lies behind the reference to "innumerable angelic hosts" which surround the throne of God.

The ideal worship in the Old Testament apocalyptic literature is that which took place in the temple. The stringed instruments connected with the sacrifical cult in the temple, John sees as harps. The censors which the priests used for burning incense in the temple, John sees as golden bowls of incense. The temple chorus of trained singers, John sees as an innumerable host of angels, the four and

twenty elders and the the four living creatures. Such was the ideal of
temple worship in the time of Ezekiel, Daniel and Isaiah. John used
allusions from Old Testament apocalptic literature in his symbols in
Revelation. The worship that John described around the throne of
God reflects not that of the church but that of the temple in Jerusalem.

> *Revelation 5:9*
> **...And they sang a new song...**

The content of the song is given. It is a song of praise to the Lamb.
The context describes a glorious sight of an innumerable company of
spiritual beings praising the Lamb. The four living creatures, the
twenty-four elders all sing the new song.[6] There was response to the
singing — as in antiphonal singing — by every created thing in
heaven and on earth.[7]

Notice the Lamb is decribed as having seven horns and seven
eyes. Notice also that the twenty-four elders are described as having
a harp and golden censors. None of this is to be taken literally. To
do so is to misunderstand the purpose of apocalyptic literature. To
take the physical description of the Lamb literally is to "de-spiritual-
ize" Jesus' present nature. To take the harps literally is to also take
the golden censors literally.

Some authors have tried to make this passage a reflection of
the liturgy of the church in Asia Minor at the end of the first century.[8]
Such does not fit the historical or Scriptural evidence. Everett
Ferguson, after investigating the testimony of early Christian writers
on the use of instrumental music by Christians concluded:

> *The conclusion that the early church did not employ*
> *instrumental music in worship does not rest, however,*
> *on inferences from silence. There are explicit statements*
> *from early Christian writers to the effect that Christians*
> *did not use instrumental music.[9]*

Several studies have been made showing that it was the synagogue,
not the temple, which provided the patterns most similar to early

Christian worship.[10] Eric Werner in studying the causes of the rejection of instrumental music in early Christian worship gives this reason.

> *Another cause against instrumental music was seen in the Christian doctrine of 'Spiritual sacrifice' (logike thysia) that disapproved of every element of sacrificial cult.*
> *Since, in Judaism at least, instrumental music was linked with the sacrifices of the Temple, the Christian reasoning quite consistently condemned all liturgical forms accessorial to sacrifice, and especially rejected instrumental performances.[11]*

The passages referring to singing in Revelation find their roots in the liturgy of the temple, not the simple, rational worship of the synagogue and the early church. Such ceremonies as burning of candles, burning of incense and the use of instrumental music are to be found in the Jewish temple worship and the contemporary liturgy of the high church, but not the Christian worship in Asia Minor in the first century.

> *Revelation 14:3*
> **...and the voice which I heard was like the sound of harpists playing on their harps. And they sang a new song before the throne...[12]**

The context again is the throne scene. Those worshipping are the hundred and forty-four thousand who have the name of the Father branded on their foreheads. Three symbols are used to describe what was heard in their worship: it was like the sound of many waters; it was like the sound of loud thunder; it was like the sound of harpists harping on their harps. None of these symbols can be taken literally any more than the number of "one hundred and forty-four thousand" can be taken literally.

The content of the new song is secret and could only be learned by the one hundred and forty-four thousand who were virgins and had the name of the Father on their foreheads. It is clear that one is not dealing with actual factual material here. Rather, it is apocalyptic literature. Symbols are to stretch the mind beyond earthly categories of human experience.

The passage says nothing about the worship of the church which takes place in time and space. John is not talking on the "wave length" of objective reality. He is using apocalyptic symbols from Old Testament literature. Such symbols find their roots in temple worship. William S. Smith comments on this passage thus:

> *Like the incense, however, the harps are only symbolic, reflecting the Jewish temple worship. The fact that both hands of the elder were occupied does not present an insuperable barrier to his prostration in worship.[13]*

This passage reflects the worship of the temple and is descriptive in a symbolic way to praise around the throne of God. It in no way suggests the practice of worship in the early church or serves as a pattern for Christian worship today.

Revelation 15:3
...And they sang the song of Moses the bond-servant of God and the song of the Lamb...

Here again there is a praise scene around the throne of God. The context shows that it was not the twenty-four elders and the four living creatures of Revelation 5:8 who were singing. Neither was it the one hundred and forty-four thousand virgins of Revelation 14:3 who were singing a new song. This time the singers were those who had been victorious over the beast and his image.

The song was not a song exalting the Lamb as in Revelation 5:8. Neither was it the secret song of Revelation 14:3. This time the song was the song of Moses and the Lamb.

The symbols of the "sea of glass" mingled with fire and "harps" are used. Perhaps the imagery here reflects the exodus of Moses from Egypt. There was the fiery sea of glass to be compared to the Red Sea through which Israel was led by a fiery cloud. There was the victory over the beast and his image to be compared to the victory over Pharaoh and his army at the Exodus.[14] There were harps of God being held by those standing by the sea of glass to be compared to musical instruments used in praise by Miriam and her company after the crossing of the Red Sea.[15] Notice the song that was sung around the sea of glass was the song of Moses as well as the song of the Lamb. The vision that John saw reflects back to worship in the wilderness but not to the worship in the church.

It should be observed that in all three passages in Revelation that "harps" are mentioned. Those who sang were "holding harps". What was heard in each case was singing — not playing. The context of both Revelation 5:9 and Revelation 15:3 give the words of the song which was sung. The singing of Revelation 14:2ff is identified as "voice". It would be impossible from these passages to show that there will be instrumental music in heaven, let alone upon the earth.

Conclusion

The very nature of spiritual beings and the fact that such were praising God in future glory would prohibit building any case for or against instrumental music in the Christian worship.

The nature of apocalyptic literature which uses shadowy symbols is too subjective in interpretation to prove or disprove any kind of doctrine or practice in the worship of the church.

The fact that all three passages draw their imagery from the Old Testament temple worship or the Exodus shows that they have nothing to say about the worship pattern of the church of Jesus Christ

ENDNOTES

[1]Revelation 5:8-10.
[2]Revelation 14:1-3.

[3]Revelation 15:2-3.
[4]See chart on page 10.
[5]Ephesians 5:19 and Colossians 3:16.
[6]Revelation 5:11.
[7]Revelation 5:13.
[8]Martin Rist, "The Revelation", *The Interpreters Bible*, Vol. XII (New York: Abington Press, 1953), p. 410.
[9]Everett Ferguson, *A Cappella Music in the Public Worship of the Church*, (Abilene, Texas: Biblical Research Press, 1972), p. 52. Documentation for this statement is to be found in the following pages of this book.
[10]Eric Werner, *The Sacred Bridge*, (New York: Columbia University Press, 1963), p. 2. W. S. Smith, *Musical Aspects of the New Testament*, (Amsterdam: University of Amsterdam, 1962), p. 1. James William McKinnon, *The Church Fathers and Musical Instruments*, (Ann Arbor: Columbia University Doctoral Dissertation, 1965), p. 1.
[11]Eric Werner, op. cit. p. 317.
[12]Revelation 14:2b-3a.
[13]William S. Smith, op. cit. p. 40.
[14]Exodus 14:27ff.
[15]Exodus 15:20ff.

CHAPTER 5

INCIDENTAL REFERENCES

There are four incidental New Testament references to singing to be considered in this chapter — Acts 16:25; I Corinthians 14:15, 26; James 5:13. The passage in Acts is an incidental example of Christians singing in crisis. The passages in I Corinthians are corrections Paul gives to the Corinthian church because they were ignoring the nature and purpose of worship in their abuse of spiritual gifts. The passage in James is an exhortation for Christians to express their happiness by singing.

The four passages are like snapshots of worship in song in the first century. They are therefore very important in understanding the nature, means and purpose of worship in song in the twentieth century. Unlike the references to singing quoted from the Old Testament in chapter three and the references in apocalyptic literature in chapter four, these passages are instructive for understanding and practicing worship in the church today. They are examples to contemporary Christians. They provide instruction for worshipping God in song.

Acts 16:25
But about midnight Paul and Silas were praying and singing hymns of praise to God, and the prisoners were listening to them.

Humneo is the word translated "to sing". Singing and praying are listed together as two closely related means of worshipping God. The context of the passage tells how Paul and Silas were put in prison at Philippi for preaching the Gospel and casting out a demon. They had been beaten and placed in the inner prison. With their backs bleeding and their feet in stocks, they expressed their deep feelings to God in song. This was no formal worship period. It was a crisis time in their lives. At such a time singing seems to be a natural thing for Christians to do.

This passage is neither a command nor an exhortation to worship in song. It is an example of spontaneous worship expressed by Christians in crisis. The time was midnight. The place was in the dungeon. The circumstances involved two men suffering pain from being beaten. But time, place and circumstances make little difference when one desires to express deep feelings to God. It is indeed an impoverished Christian life that can only worship at set times and places.

The singing of Paul and Silas was not some liturgical ritual performed out of obligation nor was it was a performance to impress the prisoners by the musical qualities of their duet. Paul and Silas' singing involved hearts full of feeling crying out to God. It is a perversion of true worship in song when such is not always the case.

When "worship services" consist of professional performances to impress the audience or set an aesthetic mood, it is not Christian worship. Worship is not a ritual performed, but it takes place in the heart of the worshipper as he expresses his deep feelings to God. The worshipper is the actor, not the audience.

James 5:13
Is anyone among you suffering? Let him pray. Is anyone cheerful? Let him sing praises.

Psallo is the word translated "to sing". In the New Testament *psallo* meant "to sing praise". This singing did not necessarily mean the singing of Old Testament Psalms. Certainly by New Testament times the word had lost its meaning "to sing with instruments". J. W.

Roberts summarizes the evidence that caused lexicographers and translators to translate the word "to sing":

> *(1) The fact that there was a growing tendency in secular Greek to use the verb in an intransitive sense with its figurative and metaphorical meaning of 'singing' (derived probably from the figurative idea of striking the vocal cords or the 'strings' of the heart); (2) the Septuagint usage where the predominant use was of the verb in the absolute to mean 'sing,' often occurring with words meaning 'to sing' in the Hebrew parallel; (3) the strong opposition in the early church (even in the stage where it was still largely a Greek-speaking church) to the use of instrumental or mechanical music.* [1]

Singing and praying are listed together again. Both are closely related in worshipping God. Songs are sometimes prayers, and prayers are sometimes sung. Many of the Old Testament Psalms are prayers or contain prayers. The contents are often very similar. They differ in that prayer is more prose and singing is more poetic. One is spoken and the other is sung.

James was encouraging the natural tendency of expressing cheerfulness in song. What better way is there to express the gratitude and joy that surges up within the heart than to sing? This must have been the thoughts in the heart of David when he penned Psalm 100.

> *Shout joyfully to the Lord, all the earth. Serve the Lord with gladness; Come before Him with joyful singing . . . Enter His gates with thanksgiving, and His courts with praise. Give thanks to Him; bless His name.* [2]

The context shows that this passage is an exhortation in the midst of a group of practical teachings on daily living. It is the beginning of several exhortations to pray. If any suffers, he is to pray. If any are sick, the elders are to pray for them. Prayer is offered for one another. Prayer avails.

Just as prayer is the response one makes to God in times of suffering, singing is a response one makes to God in times of cheerfulness.

There is nothing in this passage to suggest congregational singing. It would appear that personal private devotion was what is meant. Certainly congregational singing is not excluded. One can "sing to one another" in community as well as "pray for one another" in community. [3]

I Corinthians 14:15
What is the outcome then? I shall pray with the spirit and I shall pray with the mind also; I shall sing with the spirit and I shall sing with the mind also.

Psallo is the word translated "to sing". Again singing and praying are listed together in the text. They represent two ways of the worshipper expressing the inner feelings of his heart to God. What applied to one applied to the other.

The context of this passage shows that Paul is correcting the abuse of the spiritual gift of speaking in foreign languages that were not understood. Some of those who possessed the gift of speaking in tongues were praying and singing without understanding the words they were speaking.[4]

The one speaking did not understand the words he was saying. Paul argues that such was not worship.[5] One is not worshipping God when he says words which his mind does not understand.

The one who was listening did not understand. Paul argues that such is not edifying the church.[6] One cannot give instruction, encouragement or edification to others when they are unable to understand what is being said.

The result of this abuse of the spiritual gift of tongues was confusion.[7] Singing and praying must be understood by both the speaker and the hearer, or they do not fulfill their purposes. Understanding is important to worship.

Singing is to be done "with the spirit". This refers to the spirit of the one who is singing. In verse fifteen, Paul said, "I" will sing with the spirit. He identifies what spirit he is speaking about in verse fourteen by saying, "my" spirit. It was Paul's spirit which was involved in the praying and singing in the passage. The Holy Spirit is in the context and was the source of the spiritual gifts discussed in the passage. The language, however, identifies the "spirit" in the passage as being the spirit of man.

The spirit and the understanding of man is the source of singing and praying. The tongue is the vehicle of communication. God and the brethren are the receivers of that which is spoken in song and prayer.[8]

A basic misunderstanding of both the Greek text and the nature of worship is found in the *Living Word Paraphrase*. The passage is mistranslated to read thus:

> *I will pray in an unknown tongue and also in ordinary language that everyone understands. I will sing in an unknown tongue and also in ordinary language, so I can understand the praise I am giving.*[9]

There is absolutely no justification for such a paraphrase. This meaning has no basis in the Greek text. The context will not allow it. Paul is not discussing two kinds of worship but two elements essential to true worship — spirit and understanding.

Singing without understanding the words one is saying is not worship. It does not come from the understanding of man. Singing words that are understood but without meaning them is vain worship. Jesus condemned such:

> *You hypocrites, rightly did Isaiah prophesy of you saying, THIS PEOPLE HONORS ME WITH THEIR LIPS BUT THEIR HEART IS FAR AWAY FROM ME. BUT IN VAIN DO THEY WORSHIP ME, TEACHING AS THEIR DOCTRINES THE PRECEPTS OF MEN.*[10]

Singing words without understanding them is pagan folly. Paul makes this point in correcting the abuse of spiritual gifts on Corinth.

> *You know that when you were pagans, you were led astray to dumb idols, however you were led. Therefore I make*

> *known to you, that no one speaking by the Spirit of God*
> *says, "Jesus is accursed"; and no one can say, "Jesus is*
> *Lord", except by the Holy Spirit.*[11]

In the ecstacy of experiential worship to pagan idols, the worshippers
would surrender their will to a feeling and their understanding to
irrational behavior. In such a state they could not discern whether the
Lord or the Devil were controlling them. It is a dangerous thing to
surrender one's reason to an emotional experience and utter words
that are not understood. If the Corinthians could not understand the
words they were saying, they could not know if they were praising
Jesus or cursing Jesus.

Idol worship often had as its purpose the stimulation of the
emotions. Its goal was to obtain an experience. The worshipper used
drama, drugs, gory sacrifices, emotionally stimulating ceremonies
and different kinds of musical instruments to create these feelings.
When they obtained the experience, they believed the gods were in
them.[12]

Christian worship is distinct from pagan worship at this point.
Its purpose is not to obtain an experience, but it is to give praise to
God and to edify others. It is the "expression" of rational and genuine heart-felt praise. It is an "expression" of rational and genuine
heart-felt edification to others involved in worshipping. Pagan
worship, on the other hand, sought "impressions" from without to
stimulate emotional feelings that resulted in irrational behavior.

Paul said that singing must be "with the understanding". This
refers to the rational part of man. *Nous* is the word translated
"understanding". It refers to the mind — the reasoning part of man.
It is the same word used by Paul later in the same context:

> *However, in the church I desire to speak five words with*
> *my mind, that I may instruct others also, rather than*
> *ten thousand words in a tongue.*[13]

To separate the rational part of man from worship is to make him a
mere machine. Genuine worship requires the heart, mind and spirit.

It is impossible for a cold heart, an empty mind or an unwilling spirit to worship God. The worshipper is not edified if any one of these three elements is missing.

The abuse of the gift of tongues at Corinth has many similarities to the use of instrumental music in Christian worship.[14]

The abuse of the gift of tongues had no rational meaning to the hearer and hence did not edify. The same could be said of instrumental music in Christian worship.

The abuse of the gift of tongues was not the expression of the understanding of the worshipper and hence was not worship. The same could be said of instrumental music in Christian worship.

The abuse of the gift of tongues created excitement and stirred an emotional response on the part of the hearers much like surrendering to the ecstasy of experiential pagan worship. The same could be said of the use of instrumental music in Christian worship.

The teaching of this passage is that worship must genuinely represent both the inner spirit and reason of man. To ignore the spirit-source of worship makes words cold and empty. To ignore the understanding-source of worship would make whatever is expressed meaningless and void. Worshipping God in song must include both.

I Corinthians 14:26
What is the outcome then, brethren? When you assemble, each one has a psalm, has a teaching, has a revelation, has a tongue, has an interpretation. Let all things be done for edification.

Singing is not mentioned in this text. It is implied, however, by the phrase "each one hath a psalm". Psalms were sung; hence singing is included.

The context shows that "psalms" do not necessarily refer to the Old Testament Psalms. Paul was speaking of inspired utterances which came from the gifts of the Holy Spirit. Just as there were inspired ethical teaching, inspired revelations and inspired ability to speak in other languages, so there were also inspired psalms which came from the Holy Spirit.

It is significant that congregational singing was not always the norm for the Corinthian assembly. The text suggests "solo" singing. Notice, "each one hath a psalm" refers to the individual. This is not to suggest that congregational singing is wrong. It is reflected in other passages.[15] It does show that "solo" singing is also Scriptural and can be edifying.

This passage focuses on singing as edification. Anyone who utters a psalm must be concerned with edifying those who hear. Singing which is not understood cannot edify. Unless the hearer is able to comprehend the message of the song, it does not edify. That which does not edify should not be used. Silence is enjoined upon those who would exercise spiritual gifts which do not edify.[16]

Conclusion

Acts 16:25 shows that Christian worship in song is not limited to holy days or sacred surroundings. Paul and Silas sang hymns when their bodies were aching from a beating and their feet were in stocks. It was midnight, and they were confined to the innermost prison. Singing is a natural expression of a soul in crisis.

James 5:13 shows that Christians ought to express their cheerfulness by worshipping in song. Just as prayer is a natural expression of a Christian in suffering, singing is a natural expression of a Christian in joy.

I Corinthians 14:15 shows that singing must be motivated by the spirit and the understanding of the worshipper.

I Corinthians 14:26 shows that singing must be understood by the hearer in the assembly in order for it to edify.

Any practice of worship in song which does not include all of these elements falls short of the criteria which is set forth in the Scriptures. It cannot please God.

ENDNOTES

[1]J. W. Roberts, *A Commentary on the General Epistle of James* (Austin: R. B. Sweet Co. Inc., 1963), p. 303.

[2]Psalms 100:1-2, 4.

[3]James 5:16.

[4]For a full discussion of the nature of the gift of tongues in Corinth, see Jimmy Jividen, *Glossolalia, From God or Man?* (Fort Worth: Star Bible Publications, 1971), pp. 12-45.

[5]I Corinthians 14:14.

[6]I Corinthians 14:16-17.

[7]I Cortinthians 14:24.

[8]I Corinthians 14:14-16.

[9]*The Living Bible Paraphrased*, I Corinthians 14:15.

[10]Matthew 15:7-9.

[11]I Corinthians 12:2-3.

[12]The English word "enthusiasm" comes from the two Greek words, *en* and *theos* meaning "god in". When the pagans obtained an experience, they believed that they had "god-in-ness" or enthusiasm.

[13]I Corinthians 14:19.

[14]The abuse of tongues at Corinth consisted of an individual, who had the miraculous gift of speaking in a foreign language which he had not learned by natural means, speaking words he did not understand in an assembly of Christians who could not understand. What was done had no rational meaning to either the speaker or the hearers.

[15]See pages 85 ff

[16]I Corinthians 14:28, 30.

CHAPTER 6

BASIC PASSAGES

There are two passages which are basic to understanding the New Testament practice of worship in song. They are almost identical in content but are found in different contexts. The contexts of the passages will be considered separately. The content of both passages is so similar that it will be considered as a unit.

Ephesians 5:18-20
And do not get drunk with wine, for that is dissipation, but be filled with the Spirit, speaking to one another in psalms and hymns and spiritual songs, singing and making melody with your heart to the Lord.

The context of this passage is Paul's discussion of the Christian walk. He exhorted the Ephesian Christians to "walk no longer as the Gentiles also walk".[1] They were to "walk in love, just as Christ also loved you".[2] They were to "be careful how you walk".[3] It is in this context of discussing the Christian lifesyle in ethics, attitude and reasonableness that Paul gives an exhortation of Christian praise in song.

In the immediate context the apostle used a literary device of contrasting statements. He negated the wrong way and affirmed the right way. In verse fifteen he contrasts the "wise" with the "unwise". In verse seventeen he contrasts "foolish" with "understanding". In verse eighteen he contrasts being "drunk with wine" with being "filled with the Spirit".

This contrast between being drunk with wine and being filled with the Spirit was particularly significant in the ancient Greek world of which the Ephesians were a part. One of the gods worshipped in the Greek mysteries was Dionysus — the god of wine. His worship is described thus:

> *Thus Dionysus was worshipped under various animal forms and invoked by wild dance and song. In the frenzy of intoxication the worshippers tore living animals apart, drank their blood, and danced to the point of exhaustion. In the moment of madness thus induced they felt the spirit of the god pass into their bodies; the union so passionately desired was consummated, and the worshipper shared Dionysus' immortality.[4]*

Pagan worshippers would "get drunk" in their worship of Dionysus. They would feel "beside themselves" and purge their emotions through intoxication and the gory experience of eating the raw, warm and quivering flesh of the sacrificial animal. The experience they felt was identified with participating in the immortality of the god.

Paul contrasts being filled with the spirit of wine with being filled with the Spirit of God. Wine belonged to the irrational behavior of drunkenness. The Spirit of God brings about rational behavior in teaching and admonishing one another. Wine brings about dissipation; the Spirit of God brings about joyful praise and thanksgiving.

In this passage Paul emphasizes rational behavior which edifies. One is to be "wise", to "understand" and to be filled with the Spirit of God prompting one to "speak" to one another in song. Such conduct was a marked contrast to both the meaningless ritual of pagan ceremonies and also the irrational emotionalism of the mystery cults.

Colossians 3:15-16
And let the peace of Christ rule in your hearts, to which indeed you were called in one body; and be thankful. Let

> **the word of Christ richly dwell within you; with all
> wisdom teaching and admonishing one another with
> psalms and hymns and spiritual songs, singing with thank
> fulness in your hearts to God.**

This passage bears two similarities to the parallel passage in Ephesians. Both describe Christian conduct and attitudes. In Ephesians
Paul gives his instructions under the analogy of the "Christian walk".
In Colossians he uses the analogy of "putting off" certain things and
"putting on" certain things.

In verse five the Colossians are admonished to "put to death"
certain sins which were a part of the pagan culture. In verse eight he
refers to the sins of the tongue and admonished to "put them all
away". In verse nine they are admonished to "put off the old man
with his doings". When one becomes a Christian, the conduct of his
past sinful life is put off like a ragged, soiled garment and never put
back on again.

Beginning with verse ten Paul instructs the Colossians about
the kind of conduct and attitudes they are to "put on" as Christians.
In verse ten they are to "put on the new man". In verse fourteen they
are to "put on love".

After the "putting off" and "putting on" admonitions, Paul
gave two exhortations: "Let the peace of Christ rule in your hearts"
and "Let the word of Christ richly dwell within you".[5] When the
peace of Christ is in one's heart, he will be thankful. When the word
of Christ is in one's heart, he will teach and admonish in song. The
context of this passage emphasizes an inward attitude of thanksgiving
which finds its natural expression in songs of praise.

One of the errors refuted by Paul in Colossians was a type of
asceticism thought to be connected with Gnosticism. Its rigid rules
are reflected in one of Paul's statements.

*If you have died with Christ to the elementary principles
of the world, why, as if you were living in the world, do
you submit yourself to decrees, such as, "Do not handle,
do not taste, do not touch!" . . . These are matters which*

have, to be sure, the appearance of wisdom in self-made religion and self-abasement and severe treatment of the body, but are of no value against fleshly indulgence.[6]

In refuting this negative, gloomy and egocentric asceticism, Paul gives an exhortation to sing.

Christianity is not a heartless, cold, legal system in which ascetics glory in their own self denial. Neither is it arrogant individualism which causes its adherents to feel they are above the common herd. It is rather, a joyful life lived in grace with thanksgiving. Such a life expresses itself in singing.

An overall theme in Colossians is thanksgiving.[7] It is this thanksgiving that fills the Christian's heart with joy. It is this joy that motivates him to sing. With such thanksgiving[8] in one's heart he cannot help but sing praises to His name.

EPHESIANS 5:19 — COLOSSIANS 3:16

The similarities of these two passages are clearly seen when the terms or phrases are listed in parallel columns. A study of each will show the source, the purpose and the means of worshipping God in song.

Ephesians	Colossians
speaking	teaching and admonishing
to one another	one another
in psalms and hymns and	with psalms and hymns and
spiritual songs	spiritual songs
singing and making melody	singing
(*ado* and *psallo*)	(*ado*)
with your heart	in your hearts
to the Lord	to God

Phrase #1 is "speaking" in Ephesians and "teaching and admonishing" in Colossians. Speaking is that which comes from the rational part of man. It is this rational part of man that controls his will. It is his will that controls his speech.

...For the mouth speaks out of that which fills the heart.

The good man out of his good treasure brings forth what is good: and the evil man out of his evil treasure brings forth what is evil.[9]

The will of man fills the heart with either good or evil. What is in the heart is the source of what one speaks.

Both the spirit and the understanding — the will and the mind — of man is involved in worshipping.[10] Uttering words without willing them from the heart or understanding them with the mind is not acceptable worship to God. It is vain worship.[11] The worshipper must mean what he says and say what he means. The words he utters must be from a willing heart, an understanding mind and motivated by his own inner spirit.

Teaching and admonishing is for the purpose of edifying the hearers. The term "speaking" in Ephesians focuses on the subject of singing. The phrase "teaching and admonishing" in Colossians focuses on the hearers as the object of singing. Singing must not only be from the right inner motives, but it also must be that which will instruct and encourage the listeners. It is the same emphasis that Paul gives to the Corinthians when he said, "let all things be done unto edifying".[12]

Numerous songs which are sung in the church are for the purpose of edification. When they are sung with the spirit and the understanding, both the singer and the listener are strengthened.

The song that is often called the "invitation song"[13] is of this type. In such songs the singers are teaching and admonishing one another in the assembly to respond to the Gospel of Christ.

Phrase # 2 is "one to another" in Ephesians and "one another" in Colossians. This emphasizes the worshipping community. The "one anotherness" in singing is best understood by explaining some of the ways singing was done in the synagogue and the early church.

As has already been noted, many of the Old Testament Psalms were written for responsive singing. The leader would sing some phrases, and the congregation would respond in chorus. This form of singing is sometimes called responsorial singing.[14]

A good example of this is Psalm 107. A part of the Psalm which told a story would be sung by the leader and the congregation would respond with the short refrain.

Psalm 107:1-7 tells the story of God gathering the homeless wandering Jews. Verses eight and nine are the response of the assembly to this story.

> *Let them give thanks to the Lord for His lovingkindness, and for His wonders to the sons of men! For He has satisfied the thirsty soul, and the hungry soul He has filled with what is good.*[15]

Psalm 107:10-14 tells the story of God delivering the people out of the bondage of ignorance, sin and death. Verses fifteen and sixteen are the response of the assembly to this story.

> *Let them give thanks to the Lord for His lovingkindness, and His wonders to the sons of men! For He has shattered gates of bronze, and cut bars of iron asunder*[16]

The same pattern is followed throughout the Psalm. A story is told in song; a response is given in a refrain. It would appear that many of the Old Testament Psalms were written to be sung like this.

This responsorial style of singing is found in some contemporary songs. In the song "Angry Words", the soprano and alto sing the stanza and the whole congregation responds in the chorus. In doing this a lesson is taught in the stanza and an exhortation is given in the chorus.

Another type of singing common both to the synagogue and the early church was antiphonal singing.[17] This kind of singing involved the congregation being divided into two parts. One part of the congregation would sing a line or a phrase. Then the other part of the congregation would respond with either repeating what they heard or the next line of the Psalm.

Four part harmony in most of the contemporary songs is so structured that the bass, alto and tenor parts will respond to, compliment or emphasize words which have been sung by the soprano.

Unison singing was also practiced. All of the congregation would sing together in unison. There would be no "back and forth" singing or "repeating of words and phrases for emphasis". All would sing together. Many chants would be sung this way. It is a mistake to suggest that congregational singing was a development of a later age. It is historically substantiated throughout church history in different forms.[18] Its practice in the early church is reflected in the phrase, "speaking to one another in Psalms, hymns and spiritual songs".

There is an element of unity in the "one anotherness" of singing. In the same context of Colossians, Paul exhorted them to have the disposition of "bearing with one another", "forgiving each other" and "teaching and admonishing one another".[19] In Ephesians there are admonitions to "show forbearance to one another in love", to "be kind to one another", to "forgive each other" as well as "speaking to one another in psalms".[20]

A statement from Ambrose suggests this concept. Singing unites believers.[21]

> *Psalms are sung by emperors; the common people rejoice in them. Each man does his utmost in singing what will be a blessing to all. . . Psalmody unites those who disagree, makes friends of those at odds, brings together those who are out of charity with one another. Who could retain a grievance against a man with whom he has joined in singing before God? The singing of praise is the very bond of unity, when the whole people join in song. . .*[22]

The "one anotherness" would also imply communal singing. More than one person is involved. Solo singing is inferred from a statement by Paul in I Corinthians.[23] Group singing involving multiple persons is inferred from these two texts.

Phrase # 3 lists "psalms and hymns and spiritual songs" in both passages. Three words are used for songs. These categories are not absolute in their meaning.[24] The terms are used interchangeably. Jesus no doubt hymned a psalm.[25] It is evident that more than just the Old Testament Psalms were included in the meaning of *psalmos* since this word is used for an inspired song by Paul.[26]

A general meaning might be given to each of these words but such cannot be absolute. Psalms refer to the Old Testament Psalms but is not limited to them. Hymns refer to songs of praise to deity but again is not limited to such. Spiritual songs do not necessarily mean songs inspired by the Holy Spirit, but they are songs that are spiritual in their content.

Phrase # 4 is "singing" (*ado*) with Ephesians adding "making melody" (*psallo*) . As has already been shown there is no distinction made in the meaning of these words in the New Testament.[27] One does find here the only time in the New Testament that *psallo* has an instrument. The instrument is the heart.

It is not sufficient to sing with the lips. Christian worship in song is also making melody in the heart. The external words must be accompanied with the inward feelings of the heart and the rational understanding of the mind.

Such an admonition as "singing and making melody with your heart" would be needed in Ephesus. The pagan worship of Dionysus involved drunken frenzy in which reason was lost. Such an admonition would be needed at Colossae which was influenced by passive, negative and egocentric Gnosticism. Worship in song begins with a melody in the heart and finds expression in singing.

Phrase # 5 is "with your heart" in Ephesians and "in your hearts" in Colossians. All singing, no matter how meaningful the words or how beautiful the sound, is vain worship if it does not come from the heart of the worshipper. Perhaps it is on this point that the greatest emphasis should be made in discussing worship in song. It is when the source of singing and the purpose of singing is neglected that error arises.

In refuting the influence of pagan worship associated with drunkenness in Ephesians, Paul said, "singing and making melody in your heart". In refuting the influence of arrogant Gnosticism at Colossae, Paul said, "sing with thanksgiving in your hearts".

The best way, and perhaps the only way, for Christians to resist the tendency of men to make singing into a performance is to know and practice worship in song as shown in these passages.

The best way and perhaps the only way for Christians to identify and reject human counterfeits of worship is to know and practice worship in song as shown in these passages.

The best way and perhaps the only way for Christians to prevent singing from being just an interlude between the other items on the "worship program" is to know and practice worship in song as shown in these passages.

The best way and perhaps the only way for song leaders to stimulate vibrant personal expression and full participation in singing is to know and practice worship in song as shown in these passages.

The best way — really the only way — that one's worship in song will be acceptable praise to God is to know and practice worship in song as shown in these passages.

Phrase # 6 is "to the Lord" in Ephesians and "unto God" in Colossians. This phrase shows the direction of one's praise. It is not a mere liturgical duty to appease God. It is not a ritualistic ceremony to merely keep a commandment. It is not a public relation tool to win approval from the world. It is not merely a psychological purging of emotions to make one feel better. It is not merely a group dynamic approach to make everyone feel a part of the group. It is not an interlude or casual relief between the more important "acts of worship". It is worship to God!!!

Just as ancient Israel offered up sacrifices upon their altars in worshipping Jehovah, contemporary Christians offer up the sacrifice of praise in song. The book of Hebrews expresses this thought:

> *Through Him then, let us continually offer up a sacrifice of praise to God, that is, the fruit of lips that give thanks to His name.*[28]

Singing is part of the sacrificial offerings Christians make to God. God wants His sacrifices to be unblemished, unselfish and genuine.

Conclusion

A study of the New Testament texts on worship in song show the following points:

SOURCE: Heart   Ephesians 5:19

MEANS: Singing   Colossians 3:16

PURPOSES:
    *Edify one another   I Corinthians 14:26
    *Praise God   Ephesians 5:19 —
                                Colossians 3:16
    *Express inner feelings   James 5:13

CONTENTS: Ephesians 5:19 —
                                Colossians 3:16

    *Psalms
    *Hymns
    *Spiritual songs

ELEMENTS INVOLVED:
    *Authorized by God   Matthew 15:7
                                 Scriptural
    *Spirit and truth   John 4:23-24
                                 Inner and genuine
    *Spirit and understanding   I Corinthians14:15
                                 Will and mind
    *Heart   Ephesians 5:19
                                 Emotions

ENDNOTES

[1]Ephesians 4:17.
[2]Ephesians 5:2.
[3]Ephesians 5:15.
[4]W. T. Jones, *A History of Western Philosophy* (New York: Harcourt, Bruce and Company, 1952), p. 52.
[5]Colossians 3:15-16.

[6]Colossians 2:20-21, 23.

[7]Thanksgiving is in every chapter of Colossians. See 1:12; 2:7; 3:15, 16, 17; 4:2.

[8]The words translated "with thanksgiving" in NASV are *en chariti* and can more literally be translated "in grace" or "with grace".

[9]Matthew 12:34-35.

[10]See page 20 ff.

[11]Isaiah 29:13 and Matthew 15:8. See page 20.

[12]I Corinthians 14:26. See also page 51.

[13]Thomas H. Olbricht, "The Invitation" (*Restoration Quarterly*, Vol. 5, No. 1. First Quarter, 1961) pp. 6-16. This articles gives the historical development of the "invitation song" among both the Evangelicals and within the Restoration Movement. It arose in the camp meetings of Kentucky in the nineteenth century for the practical use of "teaching and admonishing" in evangelism.

[14]Responsorial singing involves the congregation responding to the solo singing of the cantor (leader) with such phrases as "Hallelujah", "Amen" or some such phrase.

[15]Psalms 107:8-9.

[16]Psalms 107:15-16.

[17]For a fuller discussion of the origin and development of different types of congregational singing see Jack Lewis, Everett Ferguson and Earl West, *The Instrumental Music Issue* (Nashville, Tennessee: Gospel Advocate Company, 1987), pp. 83-88.

[18]op. cit., p. 86.

[19]Colossians 3:13, 16.

[20]Ephesians 4:2, 32; 5:19.

[21]*On Psalms 1, Exposition 9.*

[22]As quoted by Everett Ferguson, *A Cappella Music in the Public Worship of the Church* (Abilene, Texas: Biblical Research Press, 1972), pp. 51-52.

[23]I Corinthians 14:26. See also page 51.

[24]See page 11.

[25]Matthew 26:30. See also page 27 ff.

[26]I Corinthians 14:26. See also page 51.

[27]See page 10 ff.

[28]Hebrews 13:15.

ARGUMENTS CONSIDERED

The place of instrumental music in Christian worship has been the focus of much controversy in the church since a very early time.

The early church fathers were negative toward instrumental music.[1] There was controversy during the Reformation Period. Most Protestant denominations had controversy over its introduction into their assembly worship. Roman Catholicism still has voices of opposition to its use. In Greek Orthodoxy it has been used only recently and in very few places. In the Restoration Movement there has been violent controversy and division over its use.

In reading the documents and history of these controversies one cannot help but see that much of the focus has been on peripheral issues which have little bearing upon the scripturalness of its use. Too often the discussions have centered around party loyalty. Papers and colleges provided forums for party leaders to consolidate their position and vanquish the opposition. Many of the arguments made for the use or the non-use of instrumental music could not stand the test of time or thought. Some of these arguments will be discussed in chapters seven and eight. Chapters nine, ten and eleven seek to confine the issue of the use or non-use of instrumental music in worship to those things which are core issues.

In Section One the emphasis was upon the definition of terms. This is essential to both the understanding and communication of any topic. In Section Two the New Testament evidence is examined in its context. This is fundamental in seeking to know the will of God. Section Three will make application of this information to discover the will of God for worship in song.

The questions are sometimes asked, "What is the best argument against the use of instrumental music in worship?" and "What is the best argument for the use of instrumental music?" These are not good questions for several reasons.

First, they portray a bias and an argumentative spirit. In the quest for truth, one's mind must always be open and his heart sensitive. An honest man does not build a fence around his faith. Truth always seeks the light. Jesus taught such:

> *For everyone who does evil hates the light and does not come to the light, lest his deeds should be exposed. But he who practices the truth comes to the light, that his deeds may be manifested as having been wrought in God.*[2]

It is true that in discussing any controversial subject, one is running the risk of possessing bias and a spirit of argumentation. There is always the temptation to build a straw man and vanquish him in order to confirm one's traditionally held convictions. The genuine Bible student seeks to overcome these barriers and honestly seek truth.

Second, the question, "What is the best argument against instrumental music?" is against the rules of argumentation. One does not affirm a negative. It is not the responsibility of the one objecting to innovations to give a "thus saith the Lord". It is the responsibility of the advocates of a practice to substantiate its use. Trying to prove that instrumental music was not a part of New Testament worship in song is like trying to prove that bitter herbs were not a part of the Lord's Supper. One cannot find any passage which teaches that it is sinful to use bitter herbs in the observance of the Lord's Supper. Neither can one quote any passage which says that it is sinful to use instrumental music with worship in song.

Third, the questions are bad because they betray a negative disposition. A better question from both those who advocate instrumental music and those who oppose instrumental music would be, "What does the New Testament teach about worship in song?" One's concern should not be, "What do I like?", "What will God tolerate?" or "How can I justify what I do?" One's ultimate concern should be, "What does God want?" and "What do the Scriptures teach?"

ARGUMENTS FAVORING INSTRUMENTAL MUSIC

In this chapter six arguments will be considered which are often used by those who advocate the use of instrumental music in worship. No attempt has been made to list them in the order of their popularity.

It is interesting to note that some of these arguments are contradictory to others of the arguments. Argument # 1 which seeks to justify instrumental music on the basis of its identification as worship in the Old Testament is contrary to argument # 2 which seeks to justify it as only an aid to worship. The latter argument would deny that instrumental music is worship. To be consistent one must deny one of these arguments to affirm the other.

Old Testament Usage

Argument # 1 could be stated thus: Instrumental music was used by the Jews in Old Testament worship to God. This authorizes its use for Christians.

Certainly instrumental music was used in the worship of the Jews in the Old Testament. Nothing could be plainer. It was used along with dancing by Miriam when she led the women in a song of praise for being delivered from Pharaoh's army.[3] It was used in the temple worship. Even before the construction of the temple, David instituted it because God had commanded it. A description of Hezekiah's animal sacrifices upon the cleansing of the temple gives this description.

> *He then stationed the Levites in the house of the Lord with cymbals, with harps, and with lyres, according to the command of David and of Gad the king's seer, and of Nathan the prophet; for the command was from the Lord through His prophets. And the Levites stood with the musical instruments of David, and the priests with the trumpets. And Hezekiah gave the order to offer the burnt offering on the altar. When the burnt offering began, the song to the Lord also began with the trumpets, accompanied by the instruments of David, the king of Israel. While the whole assembly worshipped, the singers also sang and the trumpets sounded; all this continued until the burnt offering was finished.[4]*

It should be observed that such worship with instruments of music was authorized by the Lord Himself. It was not an innovation of man. It should also be observed that it was closely connected with the animal sacrifices.

Many of the Psalms were written to be accompanied with instruments of music. Such were used in praising God. Psalm 150 shows such a use which must have been associated with temple worship.[5]

> *Praise Him with the trumpet sound; Praise Him with harp and lyre. Praise Him with timbrel and dancing; Praise Him with stringed instruments and pipe. Praise Him with loud cymbals; Praise Him with resounding cymbals.[6]*

This passage shows that instrumental music was not an "aid" to Jewish temple worship. It was worship.[7] The nature of Jewish temple worship was a ritual performance by the priestly class within the temple itself. It involved many things which would have saturated the senses of those who witnessed the ceremonies.

There were richly robed priests using vessels of gold and other precious metal. There was the sweet smell of incense, the smoking of candle wicks, the odor of burning blood, hair and animal flesh. There were singers chanting their songs and musicians playing on different instruments of music. A visit to the temple would be an awesome and memorable experience.

Some have tried to suggest that even in Old Testament times instrumental music was not sanctioned by God. To support this idea they refer to a statement in Amos.

> *Woe to those who are at ease in Zion, and to those who feel secure in the mountain of Samaria, . . . Those who recline on beds of ivory and sprawl on their couches, and eat lambs from the flock and calves from the midst of the stall, who improvise to the sound of the harp, and like David have composed songs for themselves, who drink wine from sacrificial bowls while they anoint themselves with the finest of oils, Yet they have not grieved over the ruin of Joseph.[8]*

It is an abuse of the Scriptures and a perversion of the context in which it is found to make this refer to God's displeasure of instrumental music in the temple. Amos was speaking his condemnation against the idle indifference which some of Israel's leaders had over the spiritual, social and political conditions of their time. Some of these leaders were wallowing in the luxury of wealth and at the same time were buying "the helpless for money and the needy for a pair of sandals".[9]

Amos was condemning those "at ease in Zion" rather than those who played musical instruments to the accompaniment of animal sacrifices. Certainly Amos was not condemning in this passage what God had authorized in the temple worship.

Instrumental music was very much a part of the worship of the Jewish temple. Its absence in Christian worship could not be a cultural accident or a spiritual oversight. There had to be a reason for its ceasing to be a part of man's worship to God.

The reason is simply this: God did not authorize its use when He established a new covenant with His people. God did not reveal his reason. Man might guess, but God has not revealed it. God does not need to give a reason for His action. Faith follows the will of God without knowing all of the reasons God has for making his will what it is.

It is true that instrumental music was closely connected with the animal sacrifices in the temple worship. When the temple was destroyed and the animal sacrifices ceased, it would seem logical that instrumental music along with all of the other unique items of temple worship would cease also. Everett Ferguson in his book, *A Cappella Music* , deals with this question:

> *Instrumental music, therefore, was an important feature of the temple worship, and it was closely associated with its sacrificial system. Here may be the significant clue explaining the absence of instrumental music in early Christian worship. Early Christianity saw the sacrificial system and temple worship as superseded by the sacrifice of Christ and the worship of the church. When the Levitical priesthood and the sacrificial cults were abolished, naturally its accompaniments were, too.[10]*

The temple worship ceremonies were performed by professional priests to impress the people with a sense of awe as well as to worship God. In Christian worship there is no class of performing priests. All of God's people are involved in worship. In Christian worship the emphasis is on individual "expression" of devotion to God and edification to other Christians, not the individual becoming an audience to be "impressed" by ceremonies performed by others.

The end of animal sacrifices and the priestly class connected with the temple brought about a change in the nature of worship. Temple worship was external ceremonies performed by a priestly class. Such impressed those who observed them. Christian worship is the individual's expression of inward devotion. Christian worship is different in its very nature from that of the Jewish temple. Such must have been the judgement of Edward Fudge when he wrote:

> *Singing is completely in keeping with the nature of the New
> Covenant, just as mechanical instruments of every kind
> were well suited to the character of the old.*[11]

A similar argument is made for the use of instrumental music in
Christian worship from the language of the Psalms. Psalms 87 is
supposed to be a Messianic Psalm with references to the church. It
speaks of men praising God.

> *Then those who sing as well as those who play flutes
> shall say, "All my springs of joy are in you.*[12]

It is reasoned that since the Psalm refers to the church and since it
speaks of players of flutes, it follows that instrumental music is
acceptable in the church. Several things are wrong with this reasoning. First, it must be established that the Psalm is refering to the
church. Second, it must be established that the language is literal. If
these could be established then it would demand that worship take
place on Mount Zion in Jerusalem. What proves too much proves
nothing. The only thing that such an argument proves is how desperate men are to try to justify the rituals they want to practice.

To seek support for the use of instrumental music in Christian
worship because it was used in Jewish worship in the Old Testament
is an empty quest. The use of instrumental music in sacrificial
services of the temple has no more to do with Christian worship than
the brass laver in which the priests washed their hands. The fact that
the Old Testament Psalms were sung with instrumential accompaniment has no more to do with Christian worship than eating bitter
herbs in the Passover supper has to do with the Lord's Supper. To try
and justify New Testament worship with Old Testament practices is
like adding apples and elephants. They are not the same.

Use in Heaven

Argument # 2 can be stated thus: Instrumental music is justified in
Christian worship because it is going to be used in heaven. The texts

which are used to support this contention are Revelation 5:9; 14:3; 15:3. An exposition of these passages has already been given showing that they have nothing to do with Christian worship.[13]

These passages are symbolic references to the throne of God in which the 144,000 sing the new song of Moses and the Lamb. In these passages harps are mentioned in the context along with golden bowls of incense, four living creatures, a sea of glass and the name of the Father on the forehead.

To make the harps literal is to ignore the nature of apocalyptic literature.

To use this reasoning to justify instrumental music in the church would also justify the burning of incense in golden bowls and tattooing the Father's name on the foreheads of Christians.

To make these passages a reflection of first century Christian liturgy is to ignore the use of the Old Testament temple imagery in these and other apocalyptic passages.

It is significant that all of these passages say that "singing" was heard — not the playing on harps. The text says that it was "as the voice of harpers harping on their harps".[14] One cannot in a literal sense even get instrumental music accompanying singing in heaven, let alone in the church on earth.

Aid to Worship in Song

Argument # 3 can be stated thus: instrumental music is justified in Christian worship as an aid to worship in song in the same way a song book is an aid. What is the difference in having a song book aiding in following the words of the song and a piano aiding in following the music of the song? The argument suggests that neither the song book nor the piano are worship in themselves, but rather they are aids to worship.

This is not a Scriptural argument but a logical argument. It is an argument from consistency, but it cannot be ignored. One must be consistent in his theology. If a principle is used to justify one thing as an aid to worship, it cannot be ignored when another aid is introduced by the same principle.

Song books and the piano are not parallel. They cannot be considered as aids to worship on an equal basis. Nothing more than singing is done when the song book is used. Song books only aid one in accomplishing his purpose of singing. The piano or organ involves more than singing. It is not an aid to singing, but an addition to singing. Something else is done besides singing when a piano is played. Instrumental music produces something else besides and is different from singing. The song book does not.

Instrumental music produces musical sounds that are meaningless to the mind. The song book does not. Instrumental sounds may stimulate the emotions, but they do not instruct the mind.[15]

The use of instrumental music is much like the abuse of the gifts of tongues at Corinth. The sounds uttered by those who abused the gift of tongues had no rational meaning to either the one uttering them or the ones hearing them.[16] The same could be said of instrumental music in Christian worship. The music played on the organ or other instruments has no discernable instructional meaning to either the one playing or those hearing.

It has already been established that the New Testament identifies three purposes of singing.[17] Instrumental music cannot aid in the accomplishment of any of these purposes. Song books can. The three-fold purpose of singing is (1) to praise God, (2) admonish the brethren and (3) to express personal religious feelings. Instrumental music does not aid in accomplishing any of these three purposes.

Writing in *Christianity Today*, Lowell P. Beveridge notes that the use of instrumental music has been detrimental in accomplishing the real purpose of worship in song. After affirming the New Testament practice of congregational singing and the departure from this practice during the middle ages, he writes:

Not until the early days of the Reformation was the plea for congregational singing made. Wycliffe and Hus urged a return to the principles of St. Paul, and their plea was repeated with great urgency by Luther, Calvin, Crammer, and many others. . . . . In the meantime the organ had fallen into disrepute in all but the Lutheran churches, partly because of its expense, but mostly

*because it detracted the people from their worship,
obscured the words, and interfered with the liturgical
action. . . . .Toward the end of the nineteeneth century a
change began to take place in church music that involved
a turning away from the conception strongly advocated
by the Reformers and deeply embedded in the Reformation
tradition. This change of attitude . . . . . produced a
remarkable increase of interest in a more professional
attitude toward church music. . . . . . All this conspired to
undermine the Reformation victory of music for, of, and
by the people. . . . . .Whether in prayer, praise, or preaching,
it is the words that make worship uniquely Christian, and
it is primarily through the meaning of the words that
people come to understand the meaning of Christian
symbols and sacraments.[18]*

Ignoring the purposes of worship in song lead to making it a performance of professionals to entertain. This change from people worship to professional performance perverted the purpose of worship. No longer was worship the *EXPRESSION* of an individual's devotion, it became the performer's attempt to make an *IMPRESSION* on the individual through stimulating his emotions.

Instrumental music does not make one's singing more pleasing to God. God is not served by men's hands as though he needed anything.[19] God is not concerned with the excellency of the musical composition or the beauty by which it is produced. He wants the humble devotion of the heart and the simple understandable expressions coming from the understanding of the mind.[20] The finest orchestra in the world cannot contribute to the humble sacrifice of the "fruit of lips" coming from a sincere Christian heart. Christian worship is not performance oriented to please the audience. It is the feelings of the heart, the desires of the will and the understanding of the mind finding expression in songs of praise to God.

Instrumental music does not aid in accomplishing this. A piano, an organ or an orchestra cannot teach or admonish. Instead of aiding in teaching, it is a hindrance. Instrumental music directs the mind of the worshipper from the words of the song being sung. It hinders his understanding of the words being spoken. It tends to make worship more an experience of aesthetic appreciation rather than spiritual edification.

Instrumental music does not aid one in expressing his personal devotional feelings. It does not aid the congregation in expressing religious feelings. The congregation might be IMPRESSED by the beauty of instrumental music, but certainly it is impossible for instruments to EXPRESS religious feeling by the act of hearing. Instrumental music certainly is entertaining and inspirational to men, but it is not an aid to expressing worship to God.

Included in the term Psallo

Argument # 4 can be stated thus: instrumental music is justified in Christian worship because instrumental accompaniment to singing is included in the Greek word *Psallo* .

Psallo is one of the words translated "to sing" in the New Testament.[21] It is contended that *Psallo* originally meant "to pluck" and "to play an instrument" and later "to sing to the accompaniment of an instrument". Since *Psallo* is one of the words translated "to sing" in the New Testament, then instrumental accompaniment is justified and demanded.[22]

A corollary to this line of reasoning is the use of *Psalmos* in Ephesians and Colossians with reference to what Christians sing.[23] In these passages Paul enumerated psalms, hymns and spiritual songs. *Psalmos* is translated "Psalm". It is contended that this has reference to the Old Testament Psalms which were accompanied with instrumental music in the temple worship. If Psalms were sung with instrumental music in the Old Testament, why cannot the same Psalms be sung with instrumental music in Christian worship?

This is the main linguistic argument which has been set forth by those who would advocate instrumental music in Christian worship. These arguments were often used in debates around 1900 and were formally set forth by O. E. Payne in a book entitled, *Instrumental Music is Scriptural*, published in 1914.[24] A refutation of these arguments had been set forth in a book by M. C. Kurfees in 1911.[25] The same arguments have been revived in recent years in a book by Tom Burgess.[26] All three of these books have sought to line up different linguists, encyclopedists, historians and commentators to support their positions. Their methods were more that of medieval scholasticism than that of independent research. The results were often non-critical quoting from contradicting authorities. This brought confusion to the non- technical readers.

The writings of three Greek scholars have clarified the issue in recent years. J. W. Roberts, long time Greek professor at Abilene Christian University, wrote a definitive series of articles in the *Firm Foundation* in late 1969 and early 1970 showing the true meaning of *Psallo* in the New Testament period.[27] William M. Green, long time professor of Classics at the University of California in San Francisco, wrote an excellent review of *Documents of Instrumental Music* in the Restoration Quarterly in 1967.[28] Everett Ferguson brought together both the linguistic arguments and the historical arguments in his book, *A Cappella Music in the Public Worship of the Church* .[29]

It is not the purpose of this book to accumulate all of the historical and linguistic evidence for the use of *Psallo* in order to determine its meaning in the New Testament. This has been done very well by specialists in the three works listed above. It is not the purpose of this book to line up grammarians and lexicographers to support some position. This has been done and sometimes very uncritically. It is the purpose of this author to outline the issue that is involved and draw some conlusions from the evidence.

The issue involves what *Psallo* meant in the New Testament. Its original meaning was "to pluck" in classical Greek. In the LXX it referred to singing both with and without instrumental accompaniment. This is not the question. The meaning of words change in time. The question is, " What did *Psallo* mean in the New Testament?"

Authorities can be cited on both sides of the question. This is confusing to one without the training to examine the linguistic changes in history or check the sources of this change. One cannot define a word used in the New Testament by the way that it is used in Philo. J. W. Roberts shows the importance of understanding a word in its context.

> *The meaning of words is not settled by quotations from "authorities" but by the evidence produced from historical linguistics as to the meaning of terms in their context.[30]*

William Green affirms the same principle of understanding the use of a word from its own context.

> *Words are not defined by lexicons nor by authorities of any sort. They get their definition by actual usage. Words are what their users make them. If the evidence points to the absence of instrumental music in the ancient church, the lexicographer should follow the evidence of history.[31]*

Everett Ferguson has collected the linguistic historical evidence that is available for the understanding of *Psallo* in the New Testament period. He concluded that *Psallo* did not include instrumental music in the New Testament.

> *The conclusion drawn from the New Testament texts and from linguistic evidence was that instrumental music was not present in the worship of the New Testament church. This conclusion has further support in the contextual setting of the New Testament times. Jewish practice and attitudes (both Rabbinic and Hellenistic) furnish strong presumption against the presence of instrumental music in the early church.[32]*

Though *Psallo* meant "to sing with musical accompaniment" at one time in the history of the Greek language, it meant only "to sing" in the New Testament and the early church.[33]

A serious logical question comes to mind if the use of *Psallo* demands the accompaniment of instrumental music in singing. If such were true, then it would be a sin to sing a cappella.[34]

A serious problem with this argument is the lack of evidence in either the New Testament or early church history. If indeed *psallo* demanded instrumental music, why is there no evidence?

In dealing with technical discussions about the meaning of words where evidence is limited, one should be cautious. It is doubtful that any soul-saving or soul-damning doctrine would rest upon such a technical point as the meaning of the word *Psallo* at a certain time in history. It would appear that all available evidence is clear in pointing to the fact that the term meant "to sing only" in the New Testament. This certainly would be supportive evidence in rejecting instrumental music in Christian worship. This kind of evidence is cumulative and not absolute since the term is not defined within the New Testament text itself. The basic reasons for rejecting instrumental music in Christian worship rests on other evidence. The meaning of *Psallo* as defined through a historical linguistic study only confirms what can be established through other means.

A Cultural Issue

Argument # 5: Instrumental music is justified in Christian worship to the degree that one can accept it on aesthetic and psychological grounds.

This line of reasoning suggests that the synagogue, the New Testament church and the church for several centuries after the apostles did not reject instrumental music on theological grounds. They rejected it on cultural grounds. It was associated with temple worship and pagan cult worship. Christians did not want to be identified with either of these. They would have been uncomfortable in using it because it was so much a part of that which they opposed.

Robert Donalson expressed this view in an article in *Mission* . He writes:

The choice then as to whether instruments are to be used or not must be made upon the basis of aesthetic and psychological grounds, just as it was by the early church. They excluded them not so much because of some theological

> *horror, but simply because they could not maintain a truly*
> *spiritual frame of mind in the presence of instruments*
> *which to them had so many pagan connotations.*[35]

The point being made is this. If a person can accept instrumental music without it being offensive to his own cultural background, then it is all right to use it. If he cannot, then he should not.

Everett Ferguson questions this interpretation of the evidence. After reviewing the evidence himself, he writes:

> *Surely more was involved in the absence of instruments*
> *from the worship of the church than merely a negative*
> *reaction to pagan religious practice. Where we can check*
> *the early church's attitude, it does not seem to have*
> *shown such sensitivity to the culture about it. It made*
> *its decisions on religious and moral grounds.*[36]

If instrumental music were rejected by the church because of its association with pagan and Jewish religious practices, why was not singing also rejected? The early church's faith and practice was not an evolution of the culture or a reaction to the culture. Its faith and practice came from Divine revelation.

To suggest that Christian worship practices were culturally determined is to deny the uniqueness of Christianity as a revealed religion. Christianity is more than the product of the culture into which it was born or any culture since. It is a mystery revealed by God adequate for all times and all cultures and all places. Christian worship did not evolve, it was revealed. This understanding is basic. Otherwise there would be no point in discussing this or any other subject of faith or practice.

The use or non-use of instrumental music in the Restoration Movement is more than an issue of cultural expediency. Such does not take into account the bulk of material which has been published on the matter. The vast majority of the material deals with doctrinal, not cultural arguments.

David Edwin Harrell has certainly shown social influences which ran parallel to the doctrinal divisions that came about between the Disciples of Christ and churches of Christ around the turn of the century.[37] The identity he gives to churches of Christ presupposes that their religious direction and spiritual motivation came mainly from social evolution rather than doctrinal conviction. He stated:

> *The twentieth-century Churches of Christ are the spirited offspring of the religious rednecks of the post-bellum South.[38]*

This interpretative judgement does not deal with all of the facts.   It can be pointed out that division within the Disciples of Christ did to some degree follow sectional lines and to a lesser degree social and economic lines.[39] Earl West's description of the cultural climate toward the end of the nineteenth century reflects some of these cultural infleunces.

> *With the end of the war and the vast acceleration of material prosperity, together with the rapid growth of cities, the vast expansion of industrialism, and the gaint influx of rural citizens to urban centers, the era of growth set in for churches. This was especially true in northern cities which reaped the accruements of supplying a large successful army. Members of the church moved to the city-centers and shared in some of the growing wealth. With their weekly earnings as entrepreneurs or factory workers, their contributions rose with the rise of memberships, and new church buildings dotted the streets of burgeoning cities. And churches were not hesitant to compete for the most prestigious edifices. A replendent church structure without an instrument seemed strangely incongruous. The use of the instrument now possessed new inducements.[40]*

 Other factors are involved such as the influence of strong personalities and brotherhood papers. The primary factor was doctrinal differences based upon how the Scriptures were to be understood.

One group began to question the inspiration of the Scriptures. This led to a complete rejection of the Scriptures as the sole religious authority. The results can be historically observed in the Disciples of Christ.[41]

Another group questioned the prohibitive silence of the Scripture. This led to the introduction and use of instrumental music and missionary societies. The results can be historically observed in the Conservative Christian Church.[42]

A third group accepted both the inspiration of the Scriptures and the understanding of the "prohibitive silence of the Scriptures". The results can be historically observed in the churches of Christ.

The bulk of the writing concerning the use of instrumental music focuses on it being a doctrinal issue. Christians then, as in the first century, were not that sensitive to the culture about them. They made their decisions on religious and moral grounds.

Again it should be said, that the rejection of instrumental music in Christian worship does not rest upon the subjective interpretation of cultural evidence of either the first or the nineteenth century. It is doubtful that any soul-saving or soul-damning teaching would rest upon evidence which is so open to human interpretation.

The early Christians did not consider their worship practices culturally evolved, but Divinely revealed.[43]

Certainly by reading the bulk of material surrounding the discussion of instrumental music in the last century, one is able to conclude that those who wrote this material did not believe they were dealing with a cultural phenomenon but a fundamental doctrinal issue.

Still, the historical evidence is not a basic reason for the rejection of instrumental music in Christian worship. It is a support of its rejection on other grounds. It also has a cumulative effect. The claim that the use of instrumental music in Christian worship was only a cultural issue cannot be substantiated by history.

No Authority for Congregational Singing

One of the must recent arguments to be made for instrumental music in Christain worship has been formally presented by Don DeWelt.[44] The substance of the argument is that the New Testament does not authorize congregational singing at all, therefore the use of instrumental music is all right.

The reasoning used in order to establish this conclusion would be as follows.

1. There is no authority for congregational singing in the New Testament.
2. Members of the churches of Christ practice congregational singing.
3. Therefore members of churches of Christ must not believe that one must have New Testament authority for their practices.

If this conclusion is right, it follows:

1. There is no authority for the use of instrumental music in the New Testament worship.
2. Members of the Conservative Christian Church use instrumental music in worship.
3. Therefore members of the Conservative Christian Church must not believe that one must have New Testament authority for their practice.

The conclusions from this reasoning would be that neither the practices of the Conservative Christian Church nor the churches of Christ are with Scriptural authority. With this understood, they should recognize that there is no basis for division and unite. Neither should be under the delusion that there must be Scriptural authority for their practices. Neither should object to any innovations of men which are not specifically condemned in the Scriptures. Neither should be asked to give up any of their cultural traditions.

This reasoning perhaps reflects the real feelings and thinking of most in the Conservative Christian Church. Certainly it reflects the practices of their churches. With the acceptance of this argument they forsake any pretense for having Scriptural authority for their faith and practice.

Such is not true among churches of Christ. They continue to insist that "one must have a thus saith the Lord for all that he believes and practices". They insist that worship practices must have Scriptural authority.[45]

This argument gets to the heart of the issue of using instrumental music in Christian worship. It makes all other arguments which have been made obsolete, unnecessary and useless. It does not make any difference if there was instrumental music in Jewish temple worship. It is unnecessary to discuss whether or not that *Psallo* involved the use of instrumental music in the New Testament. It is useless to discuss whether or not instrumental music is in heaven or if the opposition of instrumental music in the first century were just a cultural abhorrence. If one does not have to have Scriptural authority for what he practices in Christian worship, all of these arguments are of no consequence and therefore foolish to discuss.

The fallacy of this type of reasoning is that it begins with a false premise. It is not true that there is no New Testament authority for congregational singing in the assembly. The Corinthians sang in their assemblies.[46]

It does not state what form this singing was done. When Paul stated that singing was to be done with the spirit and the understanding[47], he did not indicate whether such was done in the form of solo, antiphonal, responsoral or unison singing. It could have been any or all of these. It would have still been singing.

The text suggests that there was an expected response — from some or all of the congregation — when one prayed with the spirit and the understanding. Would not the congregation respond to singing in a similar way?

In the Christian assembly at Corinth those who sang were told to edify the congregation in their singing.

When you assemble, each one has a psalm . . . . . Let all things be done for edifying.[48]

This singing — it would appear — was inspired through spiritual gifts. It would also appear that it was done in solo. This does not prove that all singing must be solo any more than it proves that all singing must be inspired by the Holy Spirit. The apostle is teaching that all things must be done for the edification of the congregation.

Singing solo or congregational singing would fit this criterion. Instrumental music would not.

The argument is made that "one another" and "one to another" in Ephesians and Colossians do not imply congregational singing in the assembly. It is true that the context does not show this in these passages, but neither does it identify any other specific setting. The teaching is not where the singing is to be done, but how and why it is to be done. One can teach and admonish one another with group singing of a Psalm in a garden[49], with duet singing before pagans in a prison[50] or with solo singing of inspired songs in a Christian assembly[51].

Numerous references are made to Christians singing in their assemblies beginning with Pliny the Younger in about 110 A. D. References also come from Ignatius, Tertullian, Clement of Alexandria and Eusebius showing that Christians sang in their assemblies.[52] Such historical references do not prove the point, but add confirming evidence to what is reflected in the New Testament text itself.

Argument # 6 does not justify instrumental music in Christian worship, but it does do two things.

First, it shows how desperate the advocates of instrumental music are that they have to resort to ignoring the simple meaning of the New Testament text in an effort to justify their practice.

Second, it shows the real issue involved in the instrumental music discussion is whether or not one believes he must have New Testament authority for his faith and practice.

Conclusion

The five arguments which are most often used to support the use of instrumental music in Christian worship are listed above. Much more could be written on each argument. Only an outline of the argument has been given with a response. Perhaps this will bring the real issues involved in the discussion into sharper focus in later chapters.

The attempt to justify instrumental music from the Old Testament fails because it has nothing to do with Christian worship.

Surely God commanded instrumental music in temple worship along with all of the other external rituals like animal sacrifices. When the temple worship ceased, so did the use of instrumental music. It never existed in the synagogue.

The attempt to justify instrumental music from the three symbolic passages in Revelation fails because they have nothing to do with Christian worship. Apocalyptic literature taken from Old Testament symbols talking about spirit beings around the throne in heaven is no authority for Christian worship.

The attempt to justify instrumental music as an aid to worship breaks down when one asks the question, "What does it aid?" Certainly it does not aid in expressing the devotion of the heart. It does not aid in teaching in song. It does not aid in making spiritual worship more pleasing to God.

The attempt to justify instrumental music on the basis of the definition of *Psallo* in the New Testament breaks down upon the examination of the historical and linguistic evidence. Instrumental music was not involved in the meaning of *Psallo* in New Testament times.

The attempt to justify instrumental music as a cultural expedient fails when one considers that the faith and practice of the early church was based upon revealed truth, not evolved culture. Doctrinal decisions were made on grounds of revealed religion, not as a reaction to contemporary culture.

The attempt to justify instrumental music in Christian worship by denying that there is any New Testament authority for singing in the assembly fails for two reasons.

First, plain New Testament passages are either ignored or explained away.

Second, those who advocate this position are inconsistent in their own practice. They deny there is Scriptural authority for worship in song in the assemblies, but still they practice it.

What is seen in this argument is the real issue dividing the Conservative Christian Church from churches of Christ. The issue is "Does one have to have Scriptural authority for what he desires?" To answer the question with a "yes" demands instrumental music be excluded from Christian worship. To answer the question with a "no" means that instrumental music may be included in Christian worship. This latter response also allows any other inovation of man which is not specifically condemned in the New Testament.

ENDNOTES

[1]Everett Ferguson, *A Cappella Music in the Public Worship of the Church* (Abilene, Texas: Biblical Research Press, 1972), pp. 47-83. An excellent documentation and discussion of the attitude of the early church fathers toward instrumental music is given in this book.

[2]John 3:20-21.

[3]Exodus 15:20-21.

[4]II Chronicles 29:25-28.

[5]Verse 1 of this Psalm reads, "Praise the Lord! Praise God in His sanctuary".

[6]Psalms 150:3-5.

[7]I Chronicles 23:6.

[8]Amos 6:1, 4-6.

[9]Amos 8:6.

[10]Everett Ferguson, op. cit., p. 31.

[11]Edward Fudge, "A Case Against Instrumental Music in Christian Worship", *Firm Foundation* , (June 15, 1971), p. 375.

[12]Psalms 87:7.

[13]See pages 37-43.

[14]Revelation 14:2.

[15]This is not to say that musical sounds are meaningless per se. Instrumental music can produce a soothing quality to calm the soul. It can produce sounds which stimulate to action. Such is Paul's argument in I Corinthians 14:8-9. The sounds from instruments are meaningless for rational understanding like the abuse of tongues was at Corinth. Such may stimulate the emotions, but cannot instruct the mind.

[16]I Corinthians 14:14-16.

[17]See pages 15-20.

[18]Lowell R. Beveridge, "Church Music: Pop or Pro?" *Christianity Today* (March 14, 1969), pp 527-528. Lowell R. Beveridge was professor of speech and music at Virginia Theological Seminary. He holds the Ph. D. from Harvard and served 22 years as organist and choirmaster at Columbia University.

[19]Acts 17:25.

[20]This is the lesson often repeated in the Old Testament Prophets. Psalms 40:6-10; 51:16-17;

superiority of inner holiness over external ritual. Worship is the spiritual expression of the inner man to God rather than outward physical impressions which stimulate the emotions of man.

[21] See pages 10-11 for a full discussion of the words translated "to sing".

[22] A problem with this argument which cannot be solved is this: If instrumental music is included in the meaning of *Psallo* then it would be essential for instrumental music to be used any time a person *"psalloed"*. Such is not practiced or advocated by those who use this argument.

[23] Ephesians 5:19 and Colossians 3:16.

[24] O. E. Payne, *Instrumental Music is Scriptural* (Cincinnati: The Standard Publishing Co., 1914).

[25] M. C. Kurfees, *Instrumental Music in the Worship or the Greek Word Psallo* (Nashville: Gospel Advocate Co., 1911).

[26] Tom Burgess, *Documents of Instrumental Music* (Portland: Scripture Supply House, 1966).

[27] J. W. Roberts, "A Review of "Documents on Instrumental Music" *Firm Foundation* , (November 11, 1969), p. 708; (November 18, 1969), p. 727; (November 25, 1969), pp. 743-744; (October 10, 1969), pp. 648-649; (October 17, 1969), p. 663; (December 2, 1969), pp. 759, 762; (December 9, 1969), pp. 775, 778; (December 23, 1969), p. 807; (January 6, 1970), pp. 7, 13; (January 13, 1970), pp. 23, 27; (January 20, 1970), pp. 39, 44.

[28] William M Green, "Critical Review: Documents on Instrumental Music" *Restoration Quarterly*, Vol. 10, No. 2 (Second Quarter, 1967), pp. 99-104.

[29] Everett Ferguson, op. cit.

[30] J. W. Roberts, op. cit. (December 9, 1969), p. 775.

[31] William Green, op. cit. p. 101.

[32] Everett Ferguson, op. cit., p. 42.

[33] An example of this change in word meaning is found in the term "baptism". In an English dictionary the meaning would involve "sprinkling, pouring or being dipped in water". Such was not its meaning in the first century. Christians practice baptism — not according to the current meanings — but according to the original meaning of the term in the New Testament and as reflected in the practice of the first century church.

[34] Tom Burgess, op. cit. p. 117 attempts to respond to this serious defect in his position, but he fails to face the real issue.

[35] Robert P. Donalson, "Music in Worship: Ritual Practice or Spiritual Principle", *Mission*, Vol. 3, No. 9 (March 1970).

[36] Everett Ferguson, op. cit. p. 79.

[37] David Edwin Harrell, *The Social Sources of Division in the Disciples of Christ* , 1865-1890 (Atlanta, Georgia: Publishing Systems Inc., 1973).

[38] David Edwin Harrell Jr., "The Sectional Origins of the Churches of Christ", *Mission Journal*, Vol. 14. No. 2 (August, 1980), p. 9.

[39] David Edwin Harrell Jr., loc. cit.

[40] Jack Lewis, Everett Ferguson and Earl West, op. cit. p. 63.

[41]Earl West, *The Search for the Ancient Order, Vol. 2* , (Indianapolis: Earl West Religious Book Service, 1950), pp. 250-291.

[42]This group is still in the state of flux. It would appear that many within the group want to reject the "prohibitive silence of the Scriptures" on some issues like instrumental music, but are uncomfortable with other practices which are allowed by this understanding.

[43]See Colossians 3:17

[44]Don Dewelt, "Letter to the editor," *Gospel Advocate* 127 (May 16, 1985), p. 293; Don DeWelt and Lynn Hieronymus, "Have We Cut the Gordian Knot of Instrumental Music in Congregation Singing?" *One Body* 2 (July, 1985), p. 18; "The Gordian Knot of Instrumental Music, Part II, *One Body* 2 (Winter, 1985), p. 4-6.

[45]See pages 121-134 for a discussion of the hermenuetical principles which demand that there is a "prohibitive silence" in the Scriptures.

[46]I Corinthians 14:15, 26.

[47]I Corinthians 14:15.

[48]I Corinthians 14:26.

[49]Matthew 26:30.

[50]Acts 16:25.

[51]I Corinthians 14:26.

[52]Jack Lewis, Everett Ferguson and Earl West, op. cit. p. 80-83.

CHAPTER 8

ARGUMENTS FAVORING THE NON-USE OF INSTRUMENTAL MUSIC

In this chapter four arguments will be considered which are sometimes made for the non-use of instrumental music in Christian worship. Both the strengths and weakness of these arguments will be noted.

Absence in the Early Church

Argument # 1 is an argument from history. It can be stated thus: historical evidence shows that instrumental music was introduced into Christian worship centuries after the beginning of the church and must be rejected because it is a human innovation into New Testament Christianity.

A collection of historical references to Christian worship and the attitude of early leaders of the church to instrumental music is well documented in James William McKinnon's doctoral dissertation entitled *The Church Fathers and Musical Instruments* .[1] A close study of the writing of the Church Fathers through the fourth century caused him to draw these conclusions:

Early Christianity inherited its musical practices and attitudes from Judaism, especially from the Synagogue. Unlike the Temple the Synagogue employed no instruments in its services.[2] The absence of instruments did not result from antagonism toward instruments, whether the instruments of the Temple or of the Hellenistic cults, but from the simple fact that instruments had no function in the unique service of the Synagogue. . . .

One arrives then at two distinct yet related conclusions. There is the fact that early Christian music was vocal and there is the patristic polemic against instruments. The two are related in that an analysis of the polemic confirms the fact. The most important observation one makes about the numerous patristic denunciations of instruments is that they are always made within the context of obscene theatrical performances, orgiastic banquets and the like, but not within the context of liturgical music. Evidently the occasion for speaking out against instruments in church never presented itself. One can only imagine what rhetorical outbursts the introduction of instruments into church would have elicited from Fathers like Augustine, Jerome and Chrysostom.[3]

It is not the vehemence but the uniformity of the Fathers' position which has important implications for the history of music. The patristic attitude was virtually monolithic, even though it was shared by men of diverse temperament and different regional backgrounds, and even though it extended over a span of at least two centuries of accelerated development of the Church[4]

McKinnon's study is complemented by other historical studies showing that instrumental music was not used in the early church.[5] Everett Ferguson devoted a whole section of his book to the testimony of church history in understanding the non-use of instrumental music in Christian worship.[6] His conclusion from the study confirms the judgement of McKinnon.

> *The conclusion that the early church did not employ*
> *instrumental music in worship does not rest, however,*
> *on inferences from silence. There are explicit statements*
> *from early Christian writers to the effect that Christians*
> *did not use instrumental music.[7]*

Historical studies show that instrumental music was introduced centuries after the beginning of the church. It was introduced by apostate Christianity for all of the wrong reasons.

Some musicologists, while arguing that the music of the early church was vocal, also argue that there is still evidence that instruments were used in worship at different times and places. McKinnon says that the result of such attempts "has been a history of misinterpretation and mistranslation".[8]

It has been difficult to place with accuracy the date at which instrumental music was first introduced into the worship. McKinnon suggests that it first began to appear with frequency between 1000 to 1300 A. D. Even then it was not generally used to accompany singing, but it was played before and after singing.

Instrumental music in Christian worship was opposed by many of the reformers of the Protestant Reformation among whom were Erasmus, Calvin and Zwingli. It was introduced into many of the Protestant churches with great opposition.

Instrumental music was opposed by many of the leaders of the Restoration Movement in the United States. It was not used in the early restoration churches. Students of Restoration History point to the first introduction of instrumental music into the restoration churches taking place in Midway, Kentucky before 1860.[9]

The discussion of instrumental music in the restoration movement is well documented by numerous debates, tracts and books. It proved to be one of the chief causes of division between the Disciples of Christ and churches of Christ at the beginning of the twentieth century.

Historical evidence affirms that instrumental music was not used in the early church. It was introduced gradually as a supplement to singing within the Catholic Church. It was opposed by many religious reformers in the Protestant Reformation and became one of the chief points causing division in the Restoration Movement. All of these things certainly would cause one to question its use. This is cumulative evidence to cause one to want to be doubly sure that such is acceptable to God before he begins its use.

Basic opposition to instrumental music in Christian worship is not grounded in historical evidence of human conduct. Historical evidence might not always present a complete picture. The subjective human factor is involved in the interpretation of historical evidence. Even if it were established that there was never a congregation that used instrumental music from the first to the twentieth century, that would not make it right or wrong. Human practice, humanly preserved evidence and the human factor in interpreting the evidence can all be merely the "traditions of men".

Though one must highly regard scientific historical inquiry, it is not authoritative in determining the rightness of religious ritual. History can contain error. Evidence may be misunderstood. The only authority that a Christian can look to in determining his worship to God is Jesus Christ as revealed in the Scriptures.

Historical evidence argues strongly for the rejection of instrumental music in Christian worship. It, along with other evidence, is cumulative.

A Capella is the Best Music

Argument # 2 is an argument from experience. Sometimes it is expressed by the statement: "The best argument against instrumental music is good singing".

If one meant by this statement that "good singing is that which is pleasing to God, edifying to the church and a genuine expression of a devout heart", then the statement might have validity. Observation does seem to confirm that when truth is practiced, then error can find no place.

This is probably not what is meant by "good singing" in the context of one saying that it is the best argument against instrumental music. Such a one is usually referring to the pleasing musical sounds of the singing.

The quality of the musical sounds is no valid argument for either accepting or rejecting instrumental music. One could just as well say that the best argument for not using fried chicken in the Lord's Supper is that bread and grape juice tastes better. The quality of a person's voice has nothing to do with how well pleasing it is to God. The devotion of his heart and the sincerity of his mind are essential, but whether or not his voice is approved by human critics is irrelevant.

Those who sing a cappella are not in a contest with those who sing with instrumental music to see which might sound better to the trained ear. The experiences and tastes of men are vastly different. It would be quite a problem to know which would be the better. Some would like Stamps-Baxter songs; others would like the more stately hymns; still others would like the popular songs sung by university students. The tastes and musical appreciation of men are changing and contradictory and cannot be used as criteria for acceptable worship.

The experiential argument can just as well be used the other way. An advocate of Instrumental music could say, "I like to use instrumental music because it sounds so good". Such an argument is based upon subjective feeling. It is no better or worse than to argue that "good singing is the best argument against instrumental music". The tastes and the feelings of one are just as good as another.

By applying this reasoning to the extreme, one can see the folly of this argument. "Instrumental music appeals to one's musical taste." "Instrumental music covers up the drabness of the singing." "Instrumental music makes one enjoy singing more." "Instrumental music is more attractive to 'outsiders'." On and on one could go in giving personal testimony about why he feels instrumental music is better. This kind of reasoning is all experiential.

The same kind of reasoning could apply to one who wanted to add fried chicken to the bread and grape juice in the Lord's Supper.

He could say that "fried chicken appealed to his sense of taste". He could say that "fried chicken covered up the flatness of the taste of the bread and made the Lord's Supper more desirable." "Fried chicken could make one enjoy observing the Lord's Supper more." "Fried chicken is much more attractive to 'outsiders'."

An appeal to experience or taste is never a valid authority for religious practice. Good singing — referring to its pleasing sound — might sound good to others. This is not the criterion, however, by which one determines if the songs he sings are pleasing to God.

Traditional Considerations

Argument # 3 is an argument from human tradition.[10] Instrumental music should not be used in Christian worship because it has never been used by churches of Christ in the United States.

Because something was not done by our fathers is not a valid reason for rejecting it. Because something has been practiced by our fathers is not a valid reason for accepting it. Traditions must not be the religious standard that one looks to in pleasing God.

This does not mean one is to reject something because it is a custom or tradition. In fact there should be a spirit of conformity among God's people even in customs. One of the arguments Paul made to the Corinthians for their women being veiled when they prayed and prophesied was

> But if anyone is inclined to be contentious, we have no other practice, nor have the churches of God.[11]

A thing need not be rejected because it is traditional, but tradition alone cannot be a standard of conduct.

Many of those who use instrumental music in Christian worship as well as those who reject instrumental music in Christian worship do so because of human tradition. They have been reared in a fellowship and follow the practices of that fellowship. They have not made a personal decision concerning the rightness or wrongness of the practices of the fellowship of which they are a part.

Human tradition is not a valid criterion for either accepting or rejecting instrumental music in Christian worship. One whose practice is determined by such is not seeking truth. He is in a rut.

The traditional argument is the basic reason for the rejection of instrumental music in the Greek Orthodox Church. A Cappella[12] singing seems to be practiced by most Greek Orthodox Churches, not because it is Biblical, but because it is traditional. The very nature of Greek Orthodoxy is conservative.

It is no doubt true that many within the fellowship of churches of Christ reject instrumental music for traditional reasons. Their thinking is thus: "Churches of Christ have never used instrumental music; therefore it is wrong." Such thinking not only destroys the concept of perpetual restoration in churches of Christ but also is contradictory to the teachings of the Scriptures.

> *See to it that no one takes you captive through philosophy*
> *and empty deception, according to the traditions of men, . . .*
> *rather than according to Christ.[13]*

It really does not make any difference what Alexander Campbell taught, or what David Lipscomb said or what one's great grandfather believed. Human tradition is not a valid criterion for determining acceptable worship to God.

If what one's grandfather did is according to the Scriptures, then it should be followed. This should not be because one's grandfather did it, but because it is Scriptural. If what the Pope in Rome does is according to the Scripture, then one should follow it even if it is contrary to one's own tradition. The traditions of men are neutral. Justification for one's religious practice can only come from the authority of Christ as revealed in the Scriptures.

One of the major principles which motivated men in the Restoration Movement in the United States was the rejection of human traditions. Their desire was not to reject the traditions of Catholicism and Protestantism merely to establish more traditions of the Restoration Movement. Their desire was to reject all human tradition both past and present.

It is good to be a student of the Restoration Movement of the historical past, but it is far better to be a participant of the restoration movement in the hectic present. One's faith does not rest upon the judgements or the faith of our fathers. It must rest solely and wholly upon the authority of Christ as revealed in the Scriptures.

Apostolic Example

Argument # 4 is based on apostolic example. The example of the apostolic church was a cappella singing. There is no question about it. There is no apostolic example for the use of instrumental music in Christian worship.

Does the apostolic example of singing and the lack of an apostolic example for instrumental music demand a cappella singing? The question cannot be answered until one decides what is meant by "apostolic example" and "how apostolic examples teach?" These questions must be answered before either the presence or absence of apostolic example can mean anything.[14]

The term most often used in discussing the use of an apostolic example for religious authority is an "approved apostolic example".[15] What does this mean?

An approved apostolic *example* must first of all be an example. An example is an "action" taken by individuals or churches which has been recorded in the New Testament.[16] Not all examples recorded in the New Testament have Divine approval.

There are bad examples like Herod's imprisoning Peter[17], Ananias and Sapphira's lying to God[18] and Peter's refusing to eat with the Gentiles at Antioch.[19]

There are incidental neutral examples like Christians meeting in a three story building[20], going up to the temple at the hour of prayer[21] and preaching till midnight.[22]

There are examples, though not having the force of a command, that show reasonable and sensible ways churches and individuals Christians may function. The church at Antioch prayed, fasted and laid hands on Barnabas and Saul before sending them out as missionaries.[23]   A special prayer meeting was held by Christians in Jerusalem when one of their members was put in jail.[24] Christians in Jerusalem sold their property to take care of the needs of poor brethren.[25]

The mere presence of an example does not mean that it is required. Neither does the absence of an example mean that it is forbidden.

If an action is recorded in the New Testament with obvious approval, it shows that such is right in such a circumstance. A New Testament example is helpful in clarifying things a Christian may do. It does not prove the necessity of such action at all times and in all places.

If there is no New Testament example of a particular action, it does not mean that such an action would be wrong. The New Testament was not intended to include all that a Christian can do. The lack of an apostolic example does not mean exclusive authority. A particular practice cannot be condemned merely because there is no example of it in the Scriptures.[26]

An approved *apostolic* example means that an action has apostolic sanction. It must be something that was witnessed with approval by an inspired apostolic person. The fact that such an action has the approval in one context does not demand that it must have approval in every context.

A case in point is the circumcision of Timothy in one context and Paul's refusal to circumcise Titus in another context.

Titus was not circumcised because Paul refused to compromise a principle of liberty.

> *But not even Titus who was with me, though he was a*
> *Greek, was compelled to be circumcised. But it was*
> *because of the false brethren who had sneaked in to spy*
> *out our liberty which we have in Christ Jesus, in order*
> *to bring us into bondage. But we did not yield in*
> *subjection to them for even an hour, so that the truth of*
> *the gospel might remain with you.*[27]

The same apostle in another context gave a different example. Timothy was circumcised so as not to offend the Jews. Luke recorded the example and the motive behind it.

> *Paul wanted this man to go with him; and he took him and circumcised him because of the Jews who were in those parts, for they all knew that his father was a Greek.*[28]

The examples were different in the different contexts because different principles were involved. Timothy was circumcised so as to not offend the Jews. He needed to become all things to all men. Titus was not circumcised because Paul refused to compromise a point of liberty. Different examples are given by the same apostle because different principles were involved in determining the right course of action.

An *approved* apostolic example means that it has Divine sanction. It is an example contained in the New Testament which the context shows that it has the approval of inspired apostolic men as a valid way of serving God.

The contribution which was taken up by the churches in Galatia is an "approved apostolic example".[29] It was an action taken which received the approval of an inspired apostle. It was set forth as an "example" or "pattern" to be followed by others.[30] The Corinthian church is commanded to follow the "example".

> *As I directed the churches of Galatia, so do you also. . .*[31]

Not all examples from apostolic times were approved. Paul recorded the example of the Corinthians making a feast of the Lord's Supper. This did not meet apostolic approval. It was condemned.

> *But in giving this instruction, I do not praise you, because you come together not for the better but for the worse . . . Therefore when you meet together, it is not to eat the Lord's Supper.*[32]

Three things should be noted if one seeks to gain sanction for an action on the basis of an "approved apostolic example"

First, an "approved apostolic example" does not demand what one *must* do; it rather shows what one *may* do.

Second, an "approved apostolic example" must be understood in its context as to what circumstances surround it, what principles are involved in the action and if the act is incidental or basic in doing the will of God.

Third, an "approved apostolic example" can be used only in a positive way. The existence of an "approved apostolic example" can show an action has Divine sanction and may be practiced. The non-existence of an "approved apostolic example" cannot be used to show that something is a matter of indifference. One cannot prove something is right merely because the New Testament does not give an example of its being wrong.

What do these hermeneutical principles have to do with the use of instrumental music in Christian worship? Three things should be considered.

First, the absence of an "approved apostolic example" does not condemn instrumental music in Christian worship. Its rejection must rest upon other grounds.

Second, the absence of an "approved apostolic example" for instrumental music in Christian worship demands that those who approve it must find authority for it on other grounds. It is at this point that there would be strong cumulative evidence for its rejection. If an example is not given and an authority cannot be cited, on what basis can it be practiced?

Third, it is foolish to argue from the silence of the Scriptures in regard to an "approved apostolic example" in either accepting or rejecting instrumental music in Christian worship. Logic cannot sustain either position. There is not an "authoritative word of the Lord".

The Christian concerned with doing the will of God and edifying his brethren should be concerned with two things.

First, there is full and sufficient authority for worship in song. Such is plain in the New Testament. Such is agreed upon by all parties. Such must be practiced.

Second, there is no New Testament authority for instrumental music in Christian worship. Such cannot be found by commands, examples or necessary inference. Without authority from the Scriptures, it is presumptuous to add innovations which are based solely upon personal desires. The question is not "Where does the Bible condemn it?", but rather "Where does the Bible authorize it?".

Many of the discussions concerning instrumental music in worship get bogged down in "how an apostolic example teaches". The issue of instrumental music is side tracked and nearly forgotten. It is not the purpose of this book to replow the ground that has so often been covered by others. The reader is referred to other works that are more detailed and polemic.[33]

An apostolic example gives authority for what *may* be done but not necessarily for what *must* be done. One cannot argue from the silence of an apostolic example. An example: Paul "preached until midnight" at Troas shows that such *may* be done.[34] His preaching till midnight does not mean that it *must* be done.

An approved apostolic example of instrumental music in Christian worship would give authority for its use today. The absence of an apostolic example for instrumental music in Christian worship — by itself— would not forbid it. There is no apostolic example for song books.

If the context shows that an action is the approved way of fulfilling a command, then such an apostolic example is binding. This is seen in the observance of the Lord's Supper on the first day of the week. The example of the Lord's Supper being observed at Troas on the first day of the week is an apostolic example.[35] Paul gave instructions that the Lord's Supper was to be observed by the Corinthian Christians when they came together.[36] This was an apostolic teaching. Jesus commanded his disciples to observe the Lord's Supper.[37] The command of Jesus and the teachings of an apostle lay behind the apostolic example at Troas. This makes it an "approved" apostolic example. It is an example which shows apostolic approval of how to fulfill a command.

One is not to abstain from using instrumental music in Christian worship because there was no piano in the jail at Philippi any more than he is to have his feet in stocks when he sings songs. The silence involved in having no apostolic example is not binding. An example becomes authoritative only to show how a command may be fulfilled.

Again the argument from apostolic example is not binding in and of itself. One should not ignore, however, the cumulative strength of the absence of an apostolic example for using instrumental music in Christian worship. Neither should one minimize the strength of apostolic examples for a cappella singing.

The consistency of baptism being *in* water is cumulative in showing that baptism is immersion. In the same way, the consistency of singing being a cappella is cumulative in showing that such is acceptable worship to God.

Conclusion

Four arguments have been listed which are commonly used to reject instrumental music in Christian worship. Their strengths and weaknesses have been noted. Much more could be said about each of the arguments. The reader is referred to material noted in the footnotes for a fuller discussion.

The argument for rejecting instrumental music in Christian worship because of historical evidence is strong. Human history by itself is not sufficient grounds for its rejection. There is no assurance that all of the evidence is in. There is always a subjective element in the interpretation of history

The argument for rejecting instrumental music in Christian worship from experience is weak. Whether one feels the musical qualities of singing sound good or bad makes little difference as to whether it is pleasing to God.

The argument for rejecting instrumental music in Christian worship because of human traditions is not valid. Traditions of men are neutral and have no bearing upon the rightness or wrongness of a practice.

The argument for rejecting instrumental music in Christian worship because of the lack of apostolic examples is cumulative, but it is not conclusive. It is strong enough to make one want to highly question any attempt to introduce it into the worship of the church.

It should be noted that the rejection of instrumental music in Christian worship does not solely rest on any of these arguments. It is true that the cumulative evidence of these arguments would make its use highly questionable. Taken together they should be enough to cause Christians who are concerned with a broken fellowship to desist from its use. The basic reasons for the rejection of instrumental music in Christian worship will be given in chapters IX, X, and XI.

The discussing of the pros and cons of instrumental music in Christian worship is not the best way to approach this issue. It may be necessary, but the best way to approach this issue is to discuss how best to give acceptable worship in song. If this is learned, then the other would be no problem. The following positive statement should carry more weight than all of the negative arguments.

> *The best way and perhaps the only way to resist the error of instrumental music in Christian worship is to sincerely sing from an inward sense of joy — with understandable words which teach and admonish others — for the purpose of praising God.*

When this is not done, one might as well use instrumental music in worship. Undergirding and going beyond the issue of instrumental music in Christian worship is the broader issue of the very nature of worship itself. When a Christian allows worship in song to become a formal ritual of uttering lifeless and meaningless words, there can be no consistent objection to instrumental music in worship.

When, however, Christians worship from the heart — in the spirit — in truth — and with the understanding, they will not be seeking mechanical means of worship. When the real purposes of worshipping God in song are understood and practiced, the issue of instrumental music will not seem relevant. What possible value could instrumental music have in praising God? What good could come from instrumental music in teaching and admonishing in song? What purpose could be served with instrumental music in expressing the joy in the Christian heart?

When truth is not practiced, error will arise. When the good is not done, then the evil will appear. When God is not worshipped in ways He desires and approves, then men will seek to fill the worship vacuum of their souls in other ways.

ENDNOTES:

[1]James William McKinnon, *The Church Fathers and Musical Instruments* . (New York: University Microfilms, 1967). This is a doctrinal dissertation presented to Columbia University.

[2]Erik Werner, *The Sacred Bridge* (New York: Columbia University Press, 1963). This book shows the connection between the synagogue and primitive Christian worship.

[3]James William McKinnon, op. cit. quoted from Abstract.

[4]James William McKinnon, op. cit. pp. 260-261.

[5]M. C. Kurfees, *Instrumental Music in the Worship or the Greek Verb Psallo* (Nashville: Gospel Advocate Co., 1950) pp. 143-197.

[6]Everett Ferguson, op. cit., pp. 45-85.

[7]Everett Ferguson, op. cit., p. 52.

[8]James William McKinnon, op. cit. p. 261.

[9]This is documented in an article by Ben Franklin, "Instrumental Music in Churches", *American Christian Review* (February 28, 1860), p. 34. Even before this John Boggs witnessed its use in Cincinnati in 1855. See John Boggs, "City Items", *Northwestern Christian Magazine* (December, 1855), p. 191.

[10]"Tradition"— *paradosis* — is a neutral word in the New Testament. It is used in both a good and bad sense. If human traditions are meant, then the judgement of the New Testament is negative. See Matthew 15:1-6 and Colossians 2:8. If apostolic traditions are meant, then the judgement of the New Testament is positive. See II Thessalonians 2:15; 3:6-14.

[11]I Corinthians 11:16.

[12]Everett Ferguson, op. cit. p. 83, states "The very term used in musical circles for unaccompanied singing sums up the evidence of church history. A cappella comes from the Latin by way of Italian and means 'in the style of the church,' 'as is done in the church.' The classical form of church music is unaccompanied song."

[13]Colossians 2:8.

[14]J. D. Thomas, *We Be Brethren* (Abilene, Texas: Biblical Research Press, 1958), pp. 49-75 contains a good discussion of "apostolic examples". M. R. Hadwin, *The Role of*

New Testament Examples as related to Biblical Authority (Austin, Texas: Firm
Foundation Publishing House, 1974). This little 58 page book is an outgrowth of a
Master's thesis written at Abilene Christian University and is a good discussion of
the problems surrounding the use of an "apostolic example" for religious authority.

[15]M. R. Hadwin shows the historical background of this concept in the Restoration Movement. To the concept from John Locke that religious authority must come from
that which is "commanded in express words", Thomas Campbell added the ideal
of "approved precedent" in his Declaration and Address. The ambiguity of this
concept was never clarified in either the writings of Thomas or Alexander
Campbell. See M. R. Hadwin, op. cit. p. 28.

[16]J. D. Thomas defined it as "any action or attitude of any New Testament individual or
group or church, who might reasonably be considered as exemplary characters for
our conduct or attitudes." See J. D. Thomas, op. cit., p. 49.

[17]Acts 12:3.

[18]Acts 5:1-4.

[19]Galatians 2:11-14.

[20]Acts 20:9.

[21]Acts 3:1.

[22]Acts 20:7.

[23]Acts 13:1-3.

[24]Acts 12:3-16.

[25]Acts 2:32-37.

[26]This does not mean that one may practice anything and everything he desires merely
because the Scriptures do not condemn it and no apostolic example is required.
Christian conduct is determined by what the Scriptures affirm and sanction. A
"thus saith the Lord" for all one believes and practices is that for which Christians
strive. See Colossians 3:17. It is only by this that one can know he is following
the will of God. It is only by this that there can be unity among brethren.

[27]Galatians 2:3-5.

[28]Acts 16:3.

[29]I Corinthians 16:1-2.

[30]This pattern is not binding merely because it is an "example" but because there is an
apostolic command that lies behind it.

[31]I Corinthians 16:1.

[32]I Corinthians 11:17, 20.

[33]Eugene S. Smith and Julian O. Hunt, *The Smith-Hunt Debate on Instrumental Music*
(Dallas: Good News Press Inc., 1953) and G. K. Wallace and Julian O. Hunt,
Wallace-Hunt Debate (Longview, Washington: Telegraph Book Company,
1953).

[34]Acts 20:7.

[35]Acts 20:7.

[36]I Corinthians 11:17-18.

[37]I Corinthians 11:24-25.

THE REAL ISSUES

The discussion of instrumental music in Christian worship is difficult for three reasons.

First, New Testament Christians are sensitive to the many personal and painful experiences which have historically accompanied the discussion. One is hesitant to open old wounds.

Second, such a discussion deals with technical material which requires an examination of one's presuppositions, attitudes and traditions. It demands hard critical thinking.

Third, it is thought by some to be an irrelevant issue. They consider it a dead issue of the historical past which needs no further discussion. They believe other issues are far more important and should absorb one's interest.

In spite of these difficulties, it must be discussed. It is an issue that is going to be talked about and re-examined among Christians everywhere. Many in the church consider it a matter of indifference. Many more are unsure of its importance because they have never confronted it in a personal way or had occassion to study it out for themselves. There are already a few examples of its being introduced into the church in this generation.

It needs to be stated that instrumental music in worship is only an example of basic underlying differences which exist between churches of Christ, the Disciples of Christ and what is often called "the conservative Christian Church". Instrumental music is only the tip of the iceburg. Deep underlying principles of Biblical interpretation and basic philosophical presuppositions are under the surface.

This section will deal with the basic reasons for the rejection of instrumental music in Christian worship. The background for this section has already been established. Previous chapters have dealt with word studies to determine the meaning of the terms used, textual studies to determine the context in which the relevant passages are used, theological studies to determine the meaning of worship and the purposes of worship in song as well as the weaknesses and strengths of the arguments made by the different sides of the issue. Upon the foundation of these studies, one is able to understand the following reasons for rejecting the use of instrumental music in Christian worship.

There are three basic reasons. These reasons are conclusive. They get to the heart of the matter. They can not be ignored.

The first reason is a theological reason. Instrumental music does not aid or fulfill the purposes of worshipping God in song. It does not have a valid theological base.

The second reason is an hermenuetical reason. The silence of the Scriptures will not allow the introduction of that for which there is no authority from Jesus Christ.

The third reason is a practical reason. The fellowship of the body of Christ is too precious to allow its destruction by that for which there is only human authority.

Three questions must be asked. How does instrumental music serve the purposes of worship? Where is the Scriptural authority for such? Why destroy the fellowship of the body of Christ for that which all agree is non- essential?

CHAPTER 9

THE THEOLOGICAL ISSUE

Instrumental music is not worship and is in no way supplementary to or complementary to worship as taught in the New Testament.

Worship in song in the New Testament is that which comes from the person himself. It is not something performed by others to impress the worshippers.

Such comes from the worshippers as an expression of inward devotion. Worship is not something done on the outside to "impress". It comes from the inside to "express". It is the spiritual, rational, heart-felt expression of the individual.

The Nature of Worship

The practice of instrumental music in Christian worship comes from a misunderstanding of the very nature of New Testament worship. Men seem to have always tended to make worship "liturgical" rather than "personal".[1]

This de-spiritualizing of worship is in the background of Paul's description of man's digression into pagan idolatry. The first chapter of Romans describes the steps men made in falling away from the worship of the true God into the worship of idols. It all began with the neglect of spiritual worship.

First, the text tells of a time when men knew God. God revealed Himself both in nature and revelation. Men suppressed the truth that God revealed, first by their neglect and finally by their rebellion.

> *For the wrath of God is revealed from heaven against all ungodliness and unrighteousness of men, who suppress the truth in unrighteousness, because that which is known about God is evident within them; for God made it evident to them. For since the creation of the world His invisible attributes, His eternal power and divine nature, have been clearly seen, being understood through what has been made, so they are without excuse.[2]*

Second, the text tells of a time when men neglected to worship God. They did not honor Him or give thanks to Him.

> *For even though they knew God, they did not honor Him as God, or give thanks; but they became futile in their speculations, and their foolish heart was darkened. Professing to be wise, they became fools. . .[3]*

When they neglected personal spiritual worship in praise and thanksgiving, they lost the ability to reason clearly and understand in their hearts.

Third, this developed a "worship vacuum" in their soul which sought to be filled. Since it was not filled with the genuine, it became easy for the counterfeit to be accepted. Idolatry developed with all of its deception, immorality and depravity. Paul described it thus:

> *...and exchanged the glory of the incorruptible God for an image in the form of corruptible man and of birds and four-footed animals and crawling creatures. Therefore God gave them over in the lusts of their hearts to impurity, that their bodies might be dishonored among them.[4]*

Pagan worship degenerated into the worship of physical images of idols, physical lust for worship, and physical ritual to pacify their deluded sense of the divine. This happened because they first neglected true, spiritual, rational worship of the true creator God they one time knew.

The folly of pagan worship is further described in Paul's sermon at the Areopagus at Athens. Again the physical ritual without spiritual content is condemned.

> *The God who made the world and all things in it, since He is Lord of heaven and earth, does not dwell in temples made with hands; neither is He served by human hands, as though He needed anything, since He himself gives to all life and breath and all things.[5]*

God does not need animal sacrifices to eat. God does not need incense to smell. God does not need the sounds made by dead musical instruments to hear.

God is spirit! Spiritual worship, therefore must come from the heart — the mind — the spirit of man. God is not worshipped by men's hands. Pagan worship was performed by priests in ceremonial rituals to idols made with their own hands. Their gods were too small. Their worship was too shallow.

Much of the worship offered by the Jews also betrayed a basic misunderstanding of the true nature of worship. Some no doubt thought that the sacrifices and offerings which were made at the temple were needed by God in some way. Psalm 50 refutes this misconception.

> *I shall take no young bull out of your house, nor male goats out of your folds. For every beast of the forest is Mine, the cattle on a thousand hills. I know every bird of the mountains, and everything that moves in the field is Mine. If I were hungry, I would not tell you; For the world is Mine, and all it contains. Shall I eat the flesh of bulls, or drink the blood of male goats? Offer to God a sacrifice of thanksgiving, and pay your vows to the Most High.[6]*

God wants worship that comes from the inner man. Liturgical ceremonies do not impress Him, even though they might be impressive to the people who watch them. God does not need the blood of goats, the smell of incense or the sounds of musical instruments. He wants the adoration of the devout heart of man, his submissive will and his contrite spirit.

Jesus condemned the formal ritualistic worship which was without meaning. He quoted a passage from Isaiah 29:13 and applied it to the external, man-authorized and man-directed worship they practiced.

> *THIS PEOPLE HONORS ME WITH THEIR LIPS BUT THEIR HEART IS FAR FROM ME. BUT IN VAIN DO THEY WORSHIP ME, TEACHING AS THEIR DOCTRINES THE PRECEPTS OF MEN.*[7]

Worship pleasing to God must be from the heart — not just from the lips of the worshipper. God is not interested in sound as such. He wants the personal adoration of the worshipper's heart.

Worship is more than mechanical sounds that fill the air. Worship is more than an artistic production to emotionally stimulate an audience. Worship is rather a heart-felt, mind-understood and will-motivated personal expression of the individual worshipper.

In paganism of the first century, worship was orgiastic. Dancing, drinking of wine, dramatic productions, sensual ceremonies, mysterious symbolic acts, bloody sacrifices, experiential rituals as well as the playing of instrumental music was prominent.

According to the research of William Green, instrumental music seemed to have a double purpose in Greek religion. Originally it had a magical function. It would be used to summon the god or the soul of a dead person. It would be used to ward off demons or prevent ill-omened sounds from reaching the ears of the priests. In the later Greek mystery religions instrumental music, especially flutes and drums, were used to induce ecstasy or frenzy in the worshipper.

> *The worshippers of Thracian Dionysus, also known as Bacchus, engaged in orgies at night, when members of the society were seized with a divine madness as they danced to the music, and would seize an animal or perhaps even a man, who was believed to be the incarnation of the god, tear the body limb from limb, and eat it on the spot uncooked. By this sacred communion they hoped to*

> *attain union with their god, and themselves became*
> *Bacchoi.*[8]

The function of instrumental music along with other ceremonies was a performance to stimulate the emotional, non-rational response of the hearers.

Even in the temple worship at Jerusalem, the emphasis seemed to be on the awe producing performance of the priests. One can conceptionalize what it must have been like during the offering of sacrifices by the priests and Levites.

There would be the sweet aroma of incense rising from the altar of incense. The stench of fresh blood and burning flesh from the slaughtered animals filled the air in the courtyard. There would be a faint scent of the smoke rising from the candles within the walls of the temple proper. The sense of smell would be highly stimulated.

The sight of the temple itself was awesome. It was made even more so by the great expectancy that the worshippers had after coming so far to see the holy shrine of their fathers. The architecture was grandiose. The glitter of gold, silver and brass adorned the hardware and the furniture. Beautiful tapestries made from cloth finely woven into colorful patterns hung in conspicuous places. Well trained priests performed in elaborate flowing robes and were adorned with jewels and precious metal. What the worshipper saw left him with a sense of majesty and mystery.

The sounds of the temple were unforgettable. There would be the cries of animals being slain for the sacrifices. There would be the shuffle of priests moving about performing their rituals. There would be the sizzle of burning flesh and hair. Above all of this and covering all of this would be the musical performance of the singers and players of instruments. They were trained performers and their production must have lifted the emotions of those who were in the audience. A graphic literary description of what might have been is contained in the writings of T. Dewitt Talmage.

> *Can you imagine the harmony when these white-robed*
> *Levites, before the symbols of God's presence, and by*
> *smoking altars, and the candlesticks that sprang upward*

> *and branched out like trees of gold, under the wings of*
> *the cherubim, chanting the one hundred and thirty-sixth*
> *Psalm of David? You know how it was done. One part of*
> *that great choir stood up and chanted, "Oh! give thanks*
> *unto the Lord, for He is good!" Then the other part of the*
> *choir, standing in some other part of the temple, would*
> *come in with the response: "For His mercy endureth*
> *forever." Then the first part would take up the song again,*
> *and say, "Unto Him who only doeth great wonders." The*
> *other part of the choir would come in with the*
> *overwhelming response, "For His mercy endureth forever,"*
> *until in the latter part of the song, the music floated*
> *backward and forward, harmony grappling with harmony,*
> *every trumpet sounding, every bosom heaving, one part of*
> *this great white-robed choir would lift the anthem, "Oh!*
> *give thanks unto the God of heaven," and the other part of*
> *the Levite choir would come in with the response: "For*
> *His mercy endureth forever."*[9]

The instrumentation of the harp, lyre, timbrel, pipe, cymbals and other musical instruments mentioned in Psalm 150 would be a part of the magnificent production. The audience would be awed. The emotions would be saturated. The people would leave thinking they had really been to a great performance. They had been. Instrumental music was very much a part of the temple worship. Its use today is a step backward from spiritual worship to sacramentalism of temple ceremonies.

The Jewish worship in the synagogue was different. Historical evidence has already been given suggesting that the worship of the early church follows more closely the pattern of the synagogue rather than the temple.[10] The contrast between temple and synagogue worship has been made by Eric Werner.

> *The principle and outstanding element of the Temple*
> *worship was, no doubt, the sacrificial cult, executed by*
> *a highly trained staff of professional priests who held*
> *their privileged position by dynastical birthright. The*

> *Synagogue, on the other hand, was the house of prayer,*
> *meditation and, most important, of study. In the Temple,*
> *priesthood prevailed in all its heirarchic splendour; in*
> *the Synagogue, it was the scholar and layman who moulded*
> *the service into a form which has lasted, essentially*
> *unchanged, up to the present day.* [11]

It was the synagogue and not the temple that most resembles the worship authorized by Jesus and the apostles in the New Testament.[12] Its very nature was that of personal, will-motivated, heart-felt and mind-directed worship. It was a spiritual inward expression, not the reception of some kind of emotional stimuli to produce a feeling.

The same is true of Christian worship in the twentieth century. Ritualistic ceremonies of sound, sight and smell performed to induce a sense of the "numinous"[13] is not to be substituted for real, personal, spiritual worship belonging to Christians. Christian worship is different in nature than that of pagan orgiastic worship and the Jewish temple worship performance of the priests.

Christian worship is not smelling incense; it is the expression of prayer and praise. Christian worship is not existentially viewing art objects to gain a sense of awe; it is the rational understanding that comes from the Scriptures being read in understandable language. Christian worship is neither listening to an a cappella record or an organ; it is the vocal expression by meaningful words of spiritual feelings coming from the heart.

If God were desirious of priestly performances, of objects of sight, of aroma to stimulate the sense of smell, or of sound to stimulate the listening ear, it could be done mechanically. Electronic timers, tapes recorders and mechanical robots could be programed to produce ritualistic movements, musical sounds and burning incense at the right time and place. The so- called "worshipper" could still be sleeping in bed, fishing on a lake or chasing a ball on the golf course.

No matter how sweet smelling the incense or how beautiful the recorded music, it would not be worship. It would be empty, meaningless sound. The sounds are mechanical, not meaningful.

The same can be said of instrumental music in Christian worship. It makes no difference whether it is considered worship or an aid to worship. It is mechanical sound. God does not need it; He does not want it. Psalm 51 has a beautiful expression of the kind of worship God desires.

For Thou dost not delight in sacrifice, otherwise I
would give it; Thou art not pleased with burnt offering.
The sacrifices of God are a broken spirit; A broken and
a contrite heart, O God, Thou wilt not despise.[14]

God wants the worship of a heart full of devout feelings, expressed in understandable words and motivated by a living willing spirit. It is counterfeit for one to substitute liturgical rituals for individual personal worship.

Worship is personal expression, not ritual to impress. It consists of rational praise which is understood by both the worshipper and the one who hears. The nature of this kind of worship is such that it can no way be accomplished or aided through the use of instrumental music.

The Purposes of Worship

It has already been shown that the New Testament teaches a threefold purpose in worship:[15] worship is to praise God; worship is to teach and admonish the brethren; worship is to express the deep religious feelings of joy, sorrow and devotion. The use of instrumental music in Christian worship does not accomplish or aid in any of these purposes.

God is not concerned with the excellency of the musical composition or the beauty or harmony by which it is performed. He wants the humble devotion and the simple expressions of the worshipper's heart. The finest orchestra in the world cannot contribute to or enhance the sacrifice of the "fruit of lips" which comes from a thankful heart.

Does instrumental music help in teaching and admonishing brethren? Obviously not. A piano, an organ or an orchestra cannot be a help in teaching in song. Instead of making the words which are sung more understandable, it diverts the mind of the worshipper away from the words to the mechanical musical sounds. The addition of other sounds to what is being sung hinders in understanding the words which are being spoken. It tends to make worship more an aesthetic experience to stimulate the emotions rather than a spiritual act of edification.

Does instrumental music help in expressing the religious feelings of members of the congregation? Impossible. The congregation might be impressed by the beauty of a fine musical presentation, but they cannot express religious feelings by the act of hearing. Instrumental music might be entertaining and inspirational to man, but it does not accomplish or aid in accomplishing spiritual praise to God.

Conclusion

A basic lesson should be learned about worshipping God. The true means of worshipping God has never been chosen by man. It has rather been decreed by God.

Cain's sacrifice was not pleasing to God. It was not done God's way. It was not offered with a yielding faith to God's will. It was offered according to Cain's own will.[16] The same was true of the sons of Aaron, Nadab and Abihu. They offered "strange fire" which God "commanded not".[17] They did not yield their will to the commands of God, but they offered that which they willed by their own heart.

Worship to God must be personal, rational, spiritual and according to the will of God. Instrumental music in Christian worship is not involved in any of these requirements. Instrumental music does not aid one in accomplishing worship of this nature. It must be rejected because it is contrary to the very nature and purpose of worshipping God in song.

It should be noted that one must reject on the same grounds, impersonal word worship offered in a ritualistic way, even if it is a cappella. It is just as wrong to mechanically sing a cappella as it is to use mechanical instruments of music to sing.

ENDNOTES

[1]Liturgical comes from two Greek words: *leos* meaning "people" and *ergon* meaning "work". It literally means "people work". It generally refers to ritual for public worship. It seems to indicate external works of ritual to please or pacify the gods. See page 6 for a fuller discussion of its use of *leitourgea* in the New Testament.

[2]Romans 1:19-20.

[3]Romans 1:21-22.

[4]Romans 1:23-24.

[5]Acts 17:24-25.

[6]Psalms 50:9-14.

[7]Matthew 15:8-9.

[8]William M. Green, "The Church Fathers and Musical Instruments" (An unpublished paper), p. 3-4.

[9]John Rusk, *The Authentic Life of T. DeWitt Talmage* (L. G. Stahl, 1902), p. 377.

[10]See page 94.

[11]Eric Werner, *The Sacred Bridge* (New York: Columbia University Press, 1963), p. 22.

[12]Jack Lewis, Everett Ferguson and Earl West, op. cit., p. 31. Earl West notes that those making a case for the church's borrowing its worship practices from the synagogue usually draw from source long after the New Testament was completed. Borrowing could have been from the other direction also.

[13]A word coined by Rudolph Otto from the Latin, *numen* to mean the mysterious, awe inspiring, terrible, holy, sacred quality that is of Deity.

[14]Psalms 51:16-17

[15]See pages 16-20.

[16]Hebrews 11:4; Genesis 4:4.

[17]Leviticus 10:1-3.

CHAPTER 10

THE HERMENUETICAL ISSUE

The New Testament is silent about any command to use instrumental music in Christian worship.[1] The New Testament is void of any example or inference of instrumental music being used in the worship of the early church. The glaring void of apostolic examples and the roaring silence of any passage which would command or authorize the use of instrumental music in Christian worship is sufficient reason for rejecting it.[2]

This is an hermenuetical reason for rejecting instrumental music. It revolves around "how" the silence of the Scriptures must be interpreted.[3]

An Historical Perspective

The problem of how to understand the silence of the Scriptures is not new in the history of Christian thought. It was one of the basic differences between Luther and Zwingli during the Reformation Period. Zwingli held to the idea that "what the Bible does not allow is to be rejected". Luther held to the idea that "what the Bible does not reject is allowed".

The differences they had on this point of interpretation determined many of the practices of those who followed them. Luther, following the concept that what the Bible does not condemn is condoned, retained infant baptism, instrumental music and other innovations carried over from the Roman Catholic Church. Zwingli, on the other hand led a much more thorough-going reformation. Walker writes of Zwingli thus:

> *...Only that which the Bible commands or for which distinctive authorization can be found in its pages is binding and allowable. His attitude (Zwingli jj) toward the ceremonies and order of the older worship was much more radical than that of Luther.*[4]

Luther held that a thing could be unscriptural, but not antiscriptural. It would be acceptable if it were not antiscriptural. Zwingli held that if a thing were unscriptural, it was by its very nature antiscriptural.

This same tension was found in the nineteenth century Restoration Movement in the United States. Though the motto "Speak where the Bible speaks and be silent where the Bible is silent" served as a basis for the restoration ideal, it was not always clear just what was meant by the last phrase. Much has been written in order to define more clearly just what the silence of the Scriptures meant.[5] It was how the silence of the Scriptures was to be interpreted that was the underlying reason for the division of the Restoration Movement in 1906.[6] Nowhere was the importance of how one regarded the silence of the Scripture more pronounced than in the use or non-use of instrumental music.

If the silence of the Scriptures on instrumental music means nothing, then its use in Christian worship would not be wrong. One could use it because it is not condemned. The silence of the Scriptures would allow men to do what they pleased. Accepting this hermeneutical principle would place a person in the historical stream of the Disciples of Christ and the Conservative Christian Church.[7]

It should be noted that the historical division which exists in the Restoration Movement in the United States involves much more than just the use or non-use of instrumental music. It involves a basic understanding of "how" the Scriptures teach.

The instrumental music issue was not the only issue dividing the Restoration Movement. Also involved are the issues revolving around non- Biblical "denominational structure", non-Biblical societies for missions and benevolence, the non-Biblical practice of sprinkling babies as well as the non-Biblical practice of instrumental music.[8] Instrumental music in Christian worship was the most public, the most personally threatening and the most emotionally involved issue during the last decade of the nineteenth century which had at its core the silence of the Scriptures. Instrumental music in Christian worship was not the basic issue. The basic issue was "how" the silence of the Scriptures teach. The use of instrumental music is just one of the many fruits resulting from accepting a certain hermenuetical principle.[9]

If the "silence of the Scriptures" is prohibitive, then the use of instrumental music in Christian worship would be wrong. One could not use it because it was not authorized. The silence of the Scriptures would prohibit men from doing what they pleased in worshipping God. Accepting this hermeneutical principle would place one in the historical stream of the churches of Christ.

Churches of Christ stand outside the other segments of the Restoration Movement on a number of points which are centered in their acceptance of the prohibitive nature of the "silence of the Scriptures". Even within the churches of Christ there has been much tension as church leaders have sought to beat out on the firing line of controversy the limits of Biblical silence. Such issues as "Sunday Schools", "multiple cups for the Lord's Supper", "Bible School Literature" and "Church Cooperation" have all had at their core "how the silence of the Scriptures teaches".[10]

It is not the purpose of this book to replow all that has been done in the discussion of these issues. The reader is referred to other books for a first hand account of the different positions held in these controversies.

The focus of this chapter is "Does the silence of the Scriptures allow instrumental music in Christian worship?"

By What Authority?

A logical and Biblical question to ask about the use of instrumental music in Christian worship is: "Where is the authority?" One may speak of poor singing without it. One may question the prohibitive force of the lack of an apostolic example. One may try to place it in the realm of opinion. Always, there will be the demanding question: "By what authority?"

Christians today, like Peter, should be ready and eager to give authority for all one believes and practices in religion. When questioned by the Council, Peter boldly stated his authority.

> *And when they had placed them in the center, they began*
> *to inquire, "By what power, or in what name have you*
> *done this?" Then Peter, filled with the Holy Spirit,*
> *said to them, Rulers and elders of the people, if we are*
> *on trial today for a benefit done to a sick man, as how*
> *this man has been made well, let it be known, to all of*
> *you and to all the people of Israel, that by the name of*
> *Jesus Christ the Nazarene, whom you crucified, whom God*
> *raised from The dead, — by this name this man stands*
> *here before you in good health.*[11]

The Christian finds his authority in Jesus Christ. The feelings of men, the traditions of men and the opinions of men are not sufficient authority for Christian worship. One must have a "thus saith the Lord". If there is no authority from the Lord as revealed in the Scriptures, then it must be disallowed. This applies to "sprinkling babies" as an addition to baptism. This applies to "latter day revelation" as an addition to Scripture. This applies to "human organizations of denominationalism" as an addition to the simple congregational organization of the New Testament church. This applies to the establishment of a "clergy" as an addition to the priesthood of all believers in the Scriptures. This applies to "instrumental music" as an addition to the singing practiced in the New Testament church.

This rejection of human innovation is not because of legalism. Much more is involved than doing the duty of the law. It involves loyalty to a person. It is more than mere duty in performing external rituals; it is devotion to a living Person whom men are seeking to please. The motivation for what one believes and practices in religion must not rest with institutional interest, the bondage of law or the rut of tradition. The motivation is the Person of Jesus Christ. If by yielding to His Lordship one follows the institutional policies, legal language or traditional practices, so be it! No apology is necessary. One is indifferent to them one way or the other. His concern is only to follow the Lord wherever that leads.

If institutional policies and traditional practices are Scriptural, one can rejoice. If they are not, one must resist and reject them. It is Jesus Christ that one must follow, not man, his institutions, his creeds or his traditions. A Christian must be concerned with having authority for all he believes and practices because of Jesus —and nothing else.

The Silence of the Scriptures

The silence of the Scriptures may be understood in three ways: first, silence is sometimes the unrevealed will of God that a man cannot know and does not need to know; second, silence sometimes pertains to incidentals — the ways and means of doing something which is commanded in the Scriptures — but about which details are not revealed;[12] third, silence is sometimes prohibitive. It would disallow anything beyond that which is clearly revealed.

The Unrevealed
When is the silence of the Scriptures merely the unrevealed? An example of this can be seen in how to baptize a person. One knows that a believer is to be baptized in the name of the Father, Son and Holy Spirit.[13]

One understands that the purpose of baptism is to be saved, for the remission of sins and in order to receive the gift of the Holy Spirit.[14] The Bible is silent however about just what one is to say at the time the person is baptized. One cannot know this and need not know this.

There are a lot of things about which God has not spoken. They are totally unrevealed, and it would be presumptuous to try and pierce the silence of God. God has not revealed when Jesus is to come again; it is a mystery; it consists of secrets which belong only to God.[15] R. C. Bell used to say in his Bible classes, "I don't know, I don't have to know, and I'm glad I don't have to know". One must respect the silence of the Scriptures as well as the things that are clearly revealed.

The Incidental

When does the silence of the Scriptures include the incidental? An example of this can be seen in regard to the Christian assemblies. The Scriptures are silent about where Christians are to assemble. It is evident that the New Testament church assembled often.[16] It was their practice to assemble on the first day of the week to observe the Lord's Supper.[17] When they assembled, they were to make contributions to the needs of the saints according to their prosperity[18] They were exhorted not to forsake the assembling of themselves together.[19] The Bible is silent, however, about where they were to assemble. Sometimes it was done in the temple on Solomon's porch; sometimes it was in an upper room; sometimes it was in the synagogue. Nothing is said about a "church building" or a rented hall. The Bible teaches the necessity of assembling, but the location and style of building is unrevealed. Such would be incidental to obeying the command to assemble.

The Scriptures are sometimes silent about how a thing is to be done — even though it requires that it must be done. F. L. Lemley has expressed this concept clearly:

> *...it must be observed that expedients for carrying out commands inhere in the commands and we need to have no specific authorization for any expedient. But in the absence of a command there can be no authorized expedient.*[20]

One is to observe the Lord's Supper every first day of the week. What time of day, what manner of serving and who is to serve are all incidental. The Scriptures are silent about these things. Yet, all of these things must be considered. Certain judgments must be made about them before the Lord's Supper can be observed decently and orderly. These judgments are to be made by men within the limits set forth in the Scriptures. In these things there can be diversity between congregations with different cultural backgrounds and between different generations of Christians. Men are free to use their own judgment in unrevealed matters as long as it does not involve doing more or less than what is plainly taught in the Scriptures.

An example: judgment might be that the Lord's Supper be observed at 7:30 on Sunday morning. Deacons would serve the congregation with multiple trays containing individual cups. Fine! Nothing more would be done than obeying the revealed command. If, however, it was decided to add another element to the Lord's Supper, this would be another matter. If the judgment was, not only to partake of the unleavened bread and the fruit of the vine, but also to partake of bitter herbs, this would be wrong. More was done than that which was commanded.

In the first case, nothing more was done than to exercise judgment in fulfilling a command. No specific authority is needed for an expedient. The command itself authorizes every expedient possible for implementing it. In the second case, what was done went beyond the teachings of the Scriptures to institute something different. Incidental expedients are limited to the scope of the revealed command.

To go beyond the authority of Christ revealed in the Scriptures is wrong whether it be in faith or practice. It was in such a situation that John spoke so clearly in the first century.

> *Anyone who goes too far and does not abide in the teaching of Christ, does not have God; the one who abides in the teaching, he has both the Father and the Son.*[21]

When one walks ahead of Christ, he leaves God behind. If one believes and practices that for which he has no authority in the teachings of Christ, then he is without God.

The Excluded

When is the silence of the Scriptures exclusive? An example of this can be seen in infant baptism. No where does the Bible condemn infant baptism. The Scriptures are silent about it. It is rejected, not because the Bible condemns it or because it is morally wrong. It is rejected because it is without the authority of Christ as revealed in the Scriptures.

The Scriptures teach that baptism is for penitent believers; that baptism is for the remission of sins; and that baptism is immersion. Infant baptism involves none of the above. It is something different from New Testament baptism. It is because it is different that it must be excluded. The silence of the Scriptures in such a case is exclusive. There is nothing in the practice of infant baptism which is incidental to fulfilling any command of the Bible. It is outside of and different from any New Testament teaching on baptism.

The Scriptures are silent about the use of instrumental music in Christian worship. The New Testament church prayed, sang, read Scripture, proclaimed the gospel and observed the Lord's Supper. The Bible is silent, however, about worshipping God through the playing of instrumental music. This is another case in which the silence of the Scriptures is prohibitive.

When a command is given, it logically excludes all that is not involved in the command. Woody Woodrow affirms this point:

> It is true a command, statement, or word must have limited meaning, else rational discourse would be impossible. As Hoover has noted, "if a word meant everything, then it would mean nothing in particular. To mean anything, therefore, a term must **include** itself and **exclude** or **contradict** its opposite".[22]

Language is both inclusive and exclusive. If one used the term, "man", it would exclude many things. It may also include a number of things which are incidental but not stated. The use of the term "man" would exclude an animal or an inanimate object. The term "man" may include a number of incidental things which are not expressed in the term itself. It could be a red man, a black man or a white man. All of these things would not be excluded from the term "man" itself. It could be an old or young man, a tall or short man, a big or little man or a bad or good man. All of these things would not be excluded from the term "man" itself.

The inclusive and exclusive nature of a term is to be seen in the New Testament teaching, "to sing". Many things are excluded from the term; it does not include burning incense; it does not include animal sacrifices; it does not include playing instruments of music. Certain things may be included in the term. The singing may be soft or loud; the singing may be in parts for harmony — like soprano, tenor, alto and bass; the singing may be congregational or solo. All of these incidental expedients can be involved in the term itself because nothing more is done than singing.

The New Testament teaching is "to sing". This includes all that is involved in singing. There are numerous incidental expedients which may be involved in fulfilling the command. One can have a song book, use a pitch pipe to get the pitch and have a song leader. The silence of the Scriptures does not exclude them. The authority for them is to be found in the command "to sing". Nothing more is done than singing. The silence of the Scriptures is not prohibitive when what is done accomplishes that which the Scriptures authorize.

Instrumental music is not an incidental expedient in fulfilling the Scriptural teaching "to sing". It is separate from and an addition to any such teaching. In no way does it assist one in fulfilling any teaching of the Scriptures.

If the Scriptures had just taught that a Christian was "to make music" in worshipping God, then he would have been free to do this by means of instrumental music, a cappella singing or a combination of both. Such was not the case. The Christian is instructed "to sing". Singing cannot be accomplished by playing on an instrument. New Testament singing involved the heart, the mind and the spirit of the individual as well as the sound made by his voice. Instrumental music cannot be an expedient to singing.

The Bible is not silent about worshipping in song. It is silent about the use of instrumental music in worship. Instrumental music cannot be in place of, in addition to or an aid for worshipping God in song. Singing and playing of instrumental music are two different things and have two different purposes.

The force of Scriptural silence is to be discovered in the Scriptures themselves. If one finds out how inspired men regarded the silence of the Scriptures, it would be instructive on how such is to be regarded by contemporary uninspired men.

Silence was exclusive in the law that God gave to Israel. This is shown in the command against idolatry. The law given at Sinai as recorded by Moses was brief and plain. God said, "You shall have no other gods before Me".[23] This law is expanded in Deuteronomy.

> *If there is found in your midst, in any of your towns,*
> *which the Lord your God is giving you, a man or a woman*
> *who does what is evil in the sight of the Lord your God,*
> *by transgressing His covenant, and has gone and served*
> *other gods and worshipped them, or the sun or the moon*
> *or any of the heavenly host,* **which I have not commanded**
> *. . . . then you shall bring out that man or that woman who*
> *has done this evil deed, to your gates, that is the man or*
> *the woman, and you shall stone them to death.*[24]

God did not have to enumerate all of the pagan deities of Egypt and Canaan in order to teach monotheism. All that was needed was to tell them *who* they were to worship and that excluded all others.

This principle was taught in the ministry of Jesus Himself. When Jesus was tempted to fall down and worship the Devil in order that He might receive all of the kingdoms of the world, Jesus answered with a Scripture:

> *YOU SHALL WORSHIP THE LORD, YOUR GOD, AND*
> *SERVE HIM ONLY.*[25]

The Scripture Jesus quoted was from Deuteronomy. It was not an explicit statement which prohibited the worship of the Devil. It was a positive teaching stating who was to be worshipped. This excluded all others — including the Devil. The passage is thus:

> *You shall fear only the Lord your God; and you shall*
> *worship Him, and swear by His name.*[26]

The silence of the Scripture was prohibitive in this case. It was not needful that all of the gods who have ever been worshipped by men be enumerated and receive a prohibition. A positive teaching by its very nature excluded all that were not involved in it.

Moses often emphasized that a command was exclusive as well as inclusive. Israel was not to "exceed what is written".[27] With regard to a prophet saying more than God had spoken, Moses wrote:

> *But the prophet who shall speak a word presumptuously*
> *in My name **which I have not commanded** him to speak,*
> *or which he shall speak in the name of other gods, that*
> *prophet shall die.[28]*

God did not have to condemn all the false prophecies which would be spoken by men; it was sufficient to declare that all which He had not commanded were false. If what the prophets spoke did not have the authority of God behind it, then it was to be regarded as false.

With regard to Israel worshipping in ways that were sinful, Jeremiah wrote:

> *...And they built the high places of Baal that are in*
> *the valley of Ben-hinnom to cause their sons and their*
> *daughters to pass through the fire to Molech, **which I***
> ***had not commanded** them nor had it entered My mind*
> *that they should do this abomination, to cause Judah*
> *to sin.[29]*

God did not have to enumerate all of the sinful ways to worship. He instructed Israel about the right ways of worship and that excluded all other ways. It is a serious matter to do that which "God commanded not".

One of the clearest illustrations of the exclusive nature of the silence of the Scriptures is to be seen in the story of Nadab and Abihu, the sons of Aaron. They were struck dead with fire from heaven because they offered strange fire before the Lord.

> *Now Nadab and Abihu, the sons of Aaron, took their*
> *respective firepans, and after putting fire in them,*
> *placed incense on it and offered strange fire before*

> *the Lord, **which He had not commanded** them . And fire*
> *came out from the presence of the Lord and consumed*
> *them, and they died before the Lord.*[30]

It is not clear what all was involved in the sin of Nadab and Abihu. The text says that they offered "strange fire. . . .which He had not commanded them". Fire was kept perpetually burning in the brazen altar.[31] When Aaron offered the sacrifice of atonement, he was to take fire from the brazen altar and use it in offering incense on the altar of incense.

> *And he shall take a firepan full of coals of fire from*
> *upon the altar before the Lord, and two handfuls of*
> *finely ground sweet incense, and bring it inside the veil.*
> *And he shall put the incense on the fire before the Lord,*
> *that the cloud of incense may cover the mercy seat that*
> *is on the ark of the testimony, lest he die.*[32]

Perhaps Nadab and Abihu got the fire from a place other than the brazen altar, and for this reason it was called "strange fire". Whatever the nature of their sin, one thing is evident; it was something that God "had not commanded them". When God tells man what to do, it excludes all of the alternatives which men may devise.[33]

The exclusive nature of silence is shown in the practical life of the church recorded in Acts. It seemed that certain brethren had come from Jerusalem to Antioch. They were causing a schism in the church because they demanded circumcision of all of the brethren.[34] Paul and Barnabas refused to allow this innovation into the Gentile church. All parties from Antioch came to the apostles at Jerusalem to help resolve the conflict. After much discussion, the apostles, the elders and the whole church sent letters to all the churches among the Gentiles. A part of the letter reads as follows:

> *Since we have heard that some of our number to whom*
> ***we gave no instruction** have disturbed you with their words,*
> *unsettling your souls. . .*[35]

The apostles refused to let brethren bind that which did not have the authority of Jesus or the apostles behind it. Those who brought in innovations without authority were said to have "disturbed you" and "unsettled your souls". Such is the lot of all who would bring into the practice of the church anything for which Jesus or the apostles "gave no instructions".

The exclusive nature of the silence of the Scriptures is shown in Hebrews.[36] The author, in showing the priesthood of Jesus is superior to the Levitical priesthood, argues that Jesus could not be a priest on the earth since He was of the tribe of Judah.

> *For it is evident that our Lord was descended from Judah,*
> *a tribe with reference to which Moses **spoke nothing***
> *concerning priests.*[37]

This argument is not based upon some negative prohibition against the tribe of Judah being priests. It is based upon the fact that men from the tribe of Levi were to be priests and that excluded men from the tribe of Judah and all other tribes. There was no need of a proof text to say, "Thou shalt not have priests out of the tribe of Judah". A positive command excludes all things which are not included in it. The silence of the Scriptures concerning priests coming from the tribe of Judah made it impossible for Jesus to be a priest upon the earth. G. H. Lang in commenting on this passage, said:

> *Here again the writer argues from a negative. As*
> *Moses did not connect priesthood with any tribe but*
> *that of Levi, no other tribe can put forth priests under*
> *the law of Moses. Well had it been if this rule of*
> *action had prevailed among Christians, and nothing*
> *had been introduced into their service and worship*
> *which is not found in the New Testament.*[38]

The Scriptures themselves show the force of the silence of the Scriptures to be prohibitive. Israel and the early Christians took seriously the exhortation of Moses:

> *You shall not add to the word which I am commanding*
> *you, nor take away from it, that you may keep the*

commandments of the Lord your God which I command you.[39]

Conclusion

It is true that the silence of the Scriptures can mean that something is not revealed. When that is the case, it is a mystery and cannot be known. It would be presumptuous to base a matter of faith and practice upon the unknown.

It is true that the silence of the Scripture can mean that inspiration did not deem it necessary to reveal every detail in fulfilling a command. When that is the case, man's judgment can be followed as to the best way to follow the teaching or obey the command. The command cannot be changed, but a multitude of ways may be open to fulfill the command. Nothing more or less is done than is involved in the command. Incidental expedients are devised by men in obeying the command. These incidental expedients are not binding and may be changed with the culture and the needs of the times. What cannot be changed is the command itself. To attempt to justify a thing on the basis of its being an incidental expedient when it has nothing to do with fulfilling a command is more than bad theology and faulty hermenuetics; it is presumptuous pride.

It is also true that the silence of the Scriptures can be prohibitive. Silence excludes. The very nature of language demands this. The use of the Scriptures by inspired men argues for this. That which the Bible does not authorize cannot be a part of the faith and practice of those who call Jesus Lord. Man is not free to legislate where the Bible does not speak. This has been the error of all digressions. This has been the cause of most divisions. This has been the cause for the breakdown of Biblical authority.

Refusing to respect the silence of the Scriptures ultimately leads to total apostasy. It was through the refusal to respect the silence of the Scriptures that some baptize babies; others exalt a pope; others put forth new revelation; others claim charismatic gifts; others burn incense; others use instrumental music in worship. What allows one, allows all of the others. One cannot consistently reject any of these innovations if he allows just one.

The real issue should not be what does the silence of the Scriptures allow, but what does the teaching of the Scriptures authorize. One's attitude in Bible study must not focus on what one can get by with and still make heaven. His attitude should rather focus on what one can do which most assuredly is pleasing to God.

In the discussion of instrumental music in Christian worship, it is not the task of those who reject it to show that it is condemned in the Bible. It is rather the responsibility of those who advocate it to show where it is authorized in the Scriptures. Accepting this challenge should be no problem to one who believes he must have a "thus saith the Lord for all he believes and practices". It should not produce discomfort to one when he is asked, "By what authority do you do these things?" If he can give authority for his practice, it is well and good. It gives one an opportunity to affirm his faith. If he cannot give authority for his practice, it is still well and good. It exposes his error and brings him to a better understanding of the will of God.

The author's research has taught him much about worship in song as reflected in the New Testament. He has become more sensitive to the reasons that this issue has been discussed so much by those in the Restoration Movement. He is more committed to making his own worship in song the way that God wants it. He is more convinced that dialogue between those in the Conservative Christian Church and churches of Christ will produce little positive results until there is agreement on "how" the silence of the Bible teaches.

If these three questions can be answered honestly, and if future practices would be reflected in these answers, a bold step could be made in resolving this issue.

What practice has solid Scriptural authority and is reflected in the practice of the New Testament church?

What practice is most central in accomplishing the purposes of worship in song as taught in the New Testament?

What practice is in the best interest of brotherly love and most in harmony with every person's conscience?

ENDNOTES

[1]The Scriptures are not silent about singing or worship in song. There are many passages which speak of such. It is silent about the burning of incense, lighting candles and using instrumental music connected with singing.

[2]It is not the responsibility of the negative position of a disputed question to prove the point of dispute is wrong. It is rather the responsibility of the advocate to show his position is right.

[3]The idea of understanding the silence of the Scriptures as being prohibitive goes back to the New Testament as shown on pages 130-134. Tertullian so understood it as demonstrated by his statement, "What is not expressly allowed is prohibited". (Ante-Nicene Fathers, Vol. III., p. 94). In more modern times Dirk Phillips, an author of the sixteenth century said, "It is evident that whatever God has not commanded and has not instituted by express commands of Scripture, he does not want observed". See James DeForest Murch, *Christians Only* (Cincinnati: Standard Publishing, 1962), p. 15.

[4]Williston Walker, *A History of the Christian Church* (New York: Charles Scribner's Sons, 1959), p. 322.

[5]Woody Woodrow, "The Silence of Scriptures and the Restoration Movement", *Restoration Quarterly* 28:1, (First Quarter, 1985/86), pp. 27-33.

[6]In recent years a number of sociological, sectional and cultural reasons for the division in the Restoration Movement have been set forth. Such influences cannot be denied. If one reads the written material of the period from those who were involved in the division, he cannot help but see that they considered the issues to be theological ones. It was hermenuetics, how to understand the silence of the Scriptures, which was a prominent theme in the controversy which led to division. See David Edwin Harrell, Jr., *The Social Sources of Division in the Disciples of Christ, 1865-1900* (Atlanta, Georgia: Publishers Systems Inc., 1973).

[7]The Disciples of Christ and the Conservative Christian Church generally flowed together until 1968. At that time the Disciples of Christ restructured to form a distinct denomination. It has since merged with other Protestant denominations. The Conservative Christian Church refused to restructure and has remained in the traditional Restoration Movement. It should be noted that just as it was hermeneutical principles involving the authority of the "silence of the Scriptures" which led to the division of churches of Christ from the Disciples and the Christian Church, it was hermenuetical principles involving the authority of the Scriptures themselves which led to the division of the Disciples from the Christian Church.

[8]The Mormon Movement sprang out of the Restoration Movement of the early American frontier. They broke from the main stream of the movement because of their acceptance of latter day revelations such as the *Book of Mormon, The Pearl of Great Price* and *The Doctrine and Covenants* . Part of the reasoning used to justify these new revelations was the fact that the Bible is silent about any further revelation. The Bible is silent about the Book of Mormon, but such does not justify its use. The split in the Restoration Movement resulting in the Disciples of

Christ came about because of the rejection of the prohibitive silence of the Scriptures.

[9]There are some hard questions which must be answered by those in the Conservative Christian Church who practice the use of instrumental music in Christian worship if they are to be consistent in their thinking. (1) What is the basis for rejecting infant baptism if one accepts instrumental music in worship? (2) What criteria can be used to deny fellowship to those in the Disciples of Christ which advocate "open fellowship", "women preachers" and other innovations? (3) What New Testament purpose of worship can be served in the use of instrumental music?

[10]The books which most clearly confront this issue without being clouded with personal polemics are J. D. Thomas' two volumes, *We Be Brethren* (Abilene, Texas: Biblical Research Press, 1958) and *Heaven's Window* (Abilene, Texas: Biblical Research Press, 1974).

[11]Acts 4:7-10.

[12]In one sense this category cannot be called "silence". F. L. Lemley writes concerning this: "If God has spoken on either side of a proposition, that is, if He has uttered a positive precept or a negative prohibition, there is no true domain of silence." See F. L. Lemley, "God's Silence", *Firm Foundation* (May 28, 1974), p. 5. The author does not use "silence" in this sense in this manuscript.

[13]Matthew 28:19.

[14]Mark 16:16; Acts 2:38.

[15]Deuteronomy 29:29.

[16]Acts 2:46.

[17]Acts 20:7; I Corinthians 11:17-20.

[18]I Corinthians 16:1-2.

[19]Hebrews 10:24-25.

[20]F. L. Lemley, op cit., p. 5.

[21]II John 9. There is disagreement among scholars over what constitutes the "teaching of Christ" (*tei didachei tou Christou*). If *tou Christou* is an objective genative, then the meaning would be "the teaching about Christ". Such an understanding would fit the context of John refuting false teachers who denied that Jesus came in the flesh. Verse 7 would be the key to understanding this meaning. If *tou Christou* is a subjective genative, then the meaning would be "the teaching from Christ". It would involve all teaching coming from the authority of Christ whether personally or through His apostles. Such an understanding would fit the context of John refuting false teachers who rejected the commands and the word of Christ (I John 2:3-5). Verses 1-6 would be the key to this understanding. In these verses, John identifies the false teachers as those who in some way did not know, did not abide and did not walk in the truth. (See verses 1,2,4) He further identifies "walking in truth" with "walking according to His commandments". (See verses 4, 6) One cannot determine which understanding is correct from the grammar. To understanding the exact meaning of *tou Christou* one must decide whether the narrow context of the one doctrine about the person of Christ is meant or whether the broader context of all of the commands and teaching of Christ is meant. This author holds to the latter view because of the following reasons. (1) If all of the

teaching which comes by Christ's authority is meant, it would include the doctrine of Jesus coming in the flesh in the immediate context. (2) Such an understanding would fit what appears to be the general backgrounds of the Gospel of John and his epistles. In all of them there is emphasis on truth which is identified with "word of Christ" and "commandments of Christ". John was opposing false teachers who were rejecting Jesus' authoritative teachings. John emphasized the importance of the teachings which come from Christ. Jesus' teaching — word — is that which can be known and can set one free. (John 8:31-32) Jesus' teaching — sayings — will be the basis of judgement in the last day. (John 12:47-48) Jesus' teaching —- truth, commandments and word — is the basis of knowing Christ. (I John 2:3-5) (3) Such an understanding fits into the general context of the other New Testament writings about the teachings coming from the authority of Christ. (See Acts 13:12, I Timothy 6:3-5) Abraham J. Malherbe, though taking the view that this is an objective genitive, concludes that "For John it is impossible to separate the true message about God's revelation in Christ from the person of Christ". See Abraham J. Malherbe, "Through the Eye of the Needle: 'The Doctrine of Christ'", *Restoration Quarterly* 6:1 (First Quarter, 1962), p. 18.

[22]Woody Woodrow, "The Silence of the Scriptures and the Restoration Movement", *Restoration Quarterly* 28:1 (Abilene, Texas, First Quarter, 1985/86), pp. 37-38.

[23]Exodus 20:3.

[24]Deuteronomy 17:2-3, 5.

[25]Matthew 4:10.

[26]Deuteronomy 6:13.

[27]I Corinthians 4:6.

[28]Deuteronomy 18:20; see also Jeremiah 23:32; 29:23.

[29]Jeremiah 32:35. See also Jeremiah 7:31; 19:5.

[30]Leviticus 10:1-2.

[31]Leviticus 16:12-13.

[32]Leviticus 16:12-13.

[33]Numerous other Old Testament examples demonstrate that God does not tolerate men adding to, going beyond or substituting his own desires for what God has commanded. Moses was denied entrance into the land of Canaan because he presumptuously struck the rock to get water, rather than speaking to the rock as God ordered. See Exodus 17:5-7 and Numbers 20:7-13. Uzzah was struck dead because he, as a non-Levite, touched the ark of the covenant. See Exodus 3:31 and Numbers 4:15. In both cases, the sin was in doing that for which they had no authority from God.

[34]Acts 15:1-2.

[35]Acts 15:24.

[36]Besides Hebrews 7:14 discussed below, see also Hebrews 1:5 in which the author also argues from the silence of the Scriptures.

[37]Hebrews 7:14.

[38]G. H. Lang, *The Epistle to the Hebrews* (London: The Paternoster Press, 1951), pp. 119-120.

[39]Deuteronomy 4:2; 12:32.

CHAPTER 11

FELLOWSHIP ISSUE

Christian fellowship has not been strengthened through the introduction or use of instrumental music in Christian worship. It has often been the cause of broken fellowship. A multitude of church buildings in which Disciples of Christ currently meet bear witness to this. On their corner stones is still seen chiseled the term "Church of Christ". These buildings bear silent testimony to a brotherhood broken by strong willed men who decided to introduce instrumental music into Christian worship.

Divisiveness

Fellowship in the body of Christ is too precious to be broken by that for which there is no Scriptural authority. What, or should one say who, moved men to introduce that "which God commanded not" into Christian worship? What, or should one say who, moved men to disregard the convictions of their brothers in order to have what they confessed to be "non essential"?

Added to the error of introducing instrumental music into Christian worship, "which God commanded not", is an even more grievous error of dividing the body of Christ.

Where was the spirit of brotherhood which surrenders one's own rights so as not to offend a brother when the pro instrumental party demanded the use of instrumental music in the worship of the assembly? If in matters of indifference, like eating of meat, Paul admonished brethren not to offend their fellow Christians, much more in matters of Scriptural teachings should one not violate the conscience of his brothers.[1] Listen to the language of Paul regarding this issue.

> *Therefore let us not judge one another any more, but rather determine this — not to put an obstacle or a stumbling block in a brother's way.*
>
> *For if because of food your brother is hurt, you are no longer walking according to love. Do not destroy with your food him for whom Christ died.*
>
> *So then let us pursue the things which make for peace and the building up of one another. Do not tear down the work of God for the sake of food. All things indeed are clean, but they are evil for the man who eats and gives offense. It is good not to eat meat or to drink wine, or to do anything by which your brother stumbles.*[2]

Even though "eating of meats" is not a parallel issue with "instrumental music in Christian worship", this passage does express the kind of attitude one is to have toward a brother whose conscience is offended by our action.

Brotherly Love

This kind of reasoning is a sword which cuts on both sides. If it be wrong, on the basis of brotherly love, for one to force the use of instrumental music in Christian worship on other brothers, why would it not also be wrong, on the basis of brotherly love, to deny the use of instrumental music in Christian worship if other brothers wanted it? What one demands of others, he should practice himself.

There is a difference. The use of instrumental music in Christian worship by a brother who has convictions against it is sinful. This is true whether or not it be wrong in and of itself. Paul stated this principle in discussing the eating of meats.

...he who doubts is condemned if he eats, because his eating is not from faith; and whatever is not from faith is sin.[3]

To demand the use of instrumental music in Christian worship for a brother who opposes its use is to cast a stone of stumbling before him and tempt him to sin. Brotherly love does not do this.

A cappella singing in Christian worship by a brother who believes instrumental music is acceptable is not a sin. He believes he is free "to use" or "not to use" it. He is not tempted to sin by singing a cappella. He is able to feel good about it because he has demonstrated brotherly love. In such a case the brother who sings a cappella is also called on to demonstrate brotherly love. He can open his arms of fellowship and brotherly love to the brother who is unable to see anything wrong with it — but does not use it because of brotherly love. He is to receive him "not for the purpose of passing judgement on his opinions".[4]

The brother on the pro side and the brother on the con side are both asked to do the same thing. They are to demonstrate brotherly love. The brother on the pro side is asked from his vantage point to "forego his liberty". The brother on the con side is asked from his vantage point to not "pass judgement on his brother's opinion".

If instrumental music is not used in Christian worship, the results would be fellowship. The brother who believes that it is acceptable worship is asked only to give up what he regards as an opinion. The brother who sings a cappella is not being asked to conpromise his conviction.

Brothers in the church have been doing this kind of thing on other issues for generations. There are diversities in opinions in regard to dancing, divorce, evangelism and eating in the church building. This diversity has not generally caused a break in fellowship. What is the difference in these things and the use of instrumental music in Christian worship?

141

It is different because instrumental music in Christian worship is not just an item of private personal opinion. It involves the whole church.[5] There is no way that a brother can be a part of a group which uses instrumental music without compromising his convictions.

It is different because it is a physical symbol of a practice which perverts the real purpose of worship in song. Those who regard it as an error must oppose it. Jesus was angry when he saw the innovations of men connected with the temple worship. Even though the selling of oxen, sheep and doves was not specifically condemned in the Scriptures, it was wrong. Even though the argument could be made that such aided those who came from afar in their worship activities, Jesus condemned what they were doing. John records the response of Jesus and the disciples.

> ...*and to those who were selling the doves He said,*
> *"Take these things away; stop making My Father's house*
> *a house of merchandise." His disciples remembered that*
> *it was written, "ZEAL FOR THY HOUSE WILL CONSUME*
> *ME."*[6]

Just as Jesus refused to allow the innovations of men to profane what God designated as the "holy place of worship" then, so His disciples should not allow the innovations of men to profane what God has designated as a "holy means of worship" today.

It is different because it involves community activity in the Christian assembly. Activities in the Christian assembly are to edify.[7] Christian assemblies are to provoke unto love and good works.[8] The use of instrumental music does not help in either of these purposes.

The Basis of a Christian Fellowship

Fellowship in the church is not determined by one's own personal preference. It is not accomplished by the compromise of convictions. It is not attained by peace conferences of ecclesiastical parties. It is determined by God and revealed in the Scriptures. The criteria for fellowship is not determined by man, but decreed by God.

Every man is a brother who is a son of God. No Christian chooses his brother or his brotherhood. He only recognizes what has already been determined by God. Every person begotten by the Word and born of the water and spirit is a brother.[9] There are no exceptions. There are not half-brothers, step brothers or brothers-in-law. All of the rights and privileges of brotherhood belong to every child of God.

Fellowship is narrower than brotherhood. In God's family there are "erring brothers"[10] who need to be restored and "prodigal sons"[11] who need to come back to the Father's house. There are "cut off brothers"[12] who are being disciplined by the church and "counterfeit brothers" who have left the fellowship.[13] There are "brothers who sin a sin unto death"[14] who are so far removed from God that one should not even pray for them. There are "brothers who do not abide in the teaching of Christ"[15] and are not to be received into fellowship. All of the above are brothers because they have been born into God's family. They are not in fellowship with either God or the church because of their conduct.

Fellowship has nothing to do with social, racial, cultural or temperamental preferences. The wall which divided Jews and Gentiles has been broken down. The barriers between master and slave has been removed. Fellowship in Christ is based upon spiritual criteria, not physical standards.

Fellowship in Christ is triangular. It is more than a perpendicular relationship with God. It is more than a horizontal relationship with other people. It is a triangular relationship between "God, my brother and me". It is described as such by John.

> *...if we walk in the light as He Himself is in the light,*
> *we have fellowship with one another, and the blood of*
> *Jesus His Son cleanses us from all sin.*[16]

Walking in the light means fellowship with one another. It also means a relationship with God through which our sins are cleansed by the blood of Christ.

If this triangle of fellowship is broken between my brother and me, then fellowship with God is broken. This is shown in a statement of Jesus.

> *If therefore you are presenting your offering at the altar, and there remember that your brother has something against you, leave your offering there before the altar, and go your way, first be reconciled to your brothers, and then come and present your offering.*[17]

An attempt must be made to erase the estrangement between my brother and me before my sacrifice to God is acceptable.

If this triangle of fellowship is broken between God and me, then fellowship is broken between God's other children and me. I am not to be regarded as a faithful brother in God's family if I am not a faithful son of the Father. John describes this.

> *Anyone who goes too far and does not abide in the teaching of Christ, does not have God; the one who abides in the teaching, he has both the Father and the Son. If anyone comes to you and does not bring this teaching, do not receive him into your house, and do not give him a greeting; for the one who gives him a greeting participates in his evil deeds.*[18]

To "go too far" and "not abide in the teaching of Christ" is to break fellowship with God.[19] If fellowship is broken with God, then it must not be extended by any of God's children.

Cause of a Broken Fellowship

The cause of the broken fellowship between the Conservative Christian Church and churches of Christ is not based upon traditional grounds, though there are some such barriers to be overcome in restoring fellowship. This broken fellowship is not based on cultural grounds, though cultural factors have clouded the real issue at different times and in different places. This broken fellowship is not based upon the frailties and faults of church leaders though sinful attitudes and devilish spirits are to be seen in both the past and present. It has nothing to do with the desires of men; it has everything to do with loyalty to the Lord and His teachings. The cause of the broken fellowship is theological.

The die has been cast. The results are sure. If one goes too far and ceases to abide in the teachings of Christ, he does not have God on his side. If one does not have God, then Christians should not receive him as a faithful brother. To do so would be to have fellowship with an erring brother and his evil deeds.

It is evident that the use of instrumental music in Christian worship is not according to the teachings of Christ.[20] Nowhere can it be found in the Scriptures. It does not have the authority of Christ behind it. It is beyond that which is written.[21] It is not a practice that can be done "in the name of the Lord".[22] Theological necessity demands that one cannot have fellowship with those who demand its use.

It is an exercise in futility to try and resolve the broken fellowship through a better understanding of the cultural issues, historical factors and the mistakes of the past. One must understand that the basic issues are theological ones. The authority of Christ as revealed in the Scriptures is one such issue[23], which determines the use or non-use of instrumental music in Christian worship. The purpose and nature of Christian worship is another such theological issue which determines the use or non-use of instrumental music in Christian worship. The broken fellowship between brethren is another such theological issue which is a factor in determining the use and non-use of instrumental music in Christian worship. All of these issues revolve around the Lordship of Jesus Christ and our loyalty to Him. All of these issues revolve around the inspiration and authority of the Scriptures and our willingness to know and obey them.

Conclusion

Indeed, if one be concerned with genuine worship — if one be concerned with the authority of Christ as revealed in the Scriptures — if one be concerned with fellowship among all of God's children, let him joyfully surrender the use of instrumental music in Christian worship. It has been and continues to be a cancer to destroy the body of Christ.

ENDNOTES

[1]This is not to suggest that the rejection of instrumental music in Christian worship is based upon the same kind of issue as eating of meat in the early church. It is rejected on other grounds as shown in chapters IX and X. The point is that if yielding to the conscience of a brother on non-essential matters is taught in the name of brotherly love, much more would this apply in that which is regarded as essential.

[2]Romans 14:13, 15, 19-21.

[3]Romans 14:23

[4]Romans 14:1.

[5]It should be noted that it is not merely the *opinion* that instrumental music is acceptable worship which has divided the church. It is its *use* in the assembly. There are many individuals within the fellowship of the churches of Christ who have little or no conviction against the use of instrumental music in Christian worship. This *opinion* does not cause division. It is the *use* of instrumental music against the convictions of those who oppose it which has caused and still causes division.

[6]John 2:16-17.

[7]I Corinthians 14:26.

[8]Hebrews 10:24-25.

[9]I Peter 1:23; James 1:18; John 3:3,5.

[10]Galatians 6:1; James 5:19-20.

[11]Luke 15:11ff.

[12]I Corinthians 5:1-13.

[13]I John 2:15.

[14]I John 5:16.

[15]II John 9-11.

[16]I John 1:7.

[17]Matthew 5:23-24.

[18]II John 9-11.

[19]For what is involved in the teaching of Christ see footnote 21, page 137.

[20]See chapter X, pages 125 ff.

[21]I Corinthians 4:6.

[22]Colossians 3:17.

[23]A simple study of the New Testament texts shows what practices come with apostolic authority and what practices have been established by the practice of the early church. What good can be gained by doing more than that which is authorized — except the breaking of the bonds of fellowship?

SECTION V

PRACTICAL EXHORTATION

All of the previous material in this book will be of little value unless in some way individuals and groups are motivated to act upon it in a practical way. It is a big and bold step from the ideal of academics to the reality of actual practice. It has always been so. Jesus spoke of this problem with the scholars and religious leaders of His time in Matthew 23:1-4.

> . . . *The scribes and the Pharisees have seated themselves in the chair of Moses; therefore all that they tell you, do and observe, but do not do according to their deeds; for they say things, and do not do them. And they tie up heavy loads, and lay them on men's shoulders; but they themselves are unwilling to move them with so much as a finger.*

It is easier to say than to do. It is easier to put forth a theory than it is to put it into practice. It is easier to ask of another more than one is willing to do himself.

The purpose of this last section is to challenge all those in the historical Restoration Movement to go back to the basic principles which led great religious leaders more than 150 years ago to seek to become the ideal church as revealed in the Scriptures.

This demands a fresh study of the purpose and pattern of New Testament worship in song. This demands a surrender of human traditions and a breakdown of party lines. This demands an unselfish agape love which places a brother's feelings over what one considers personal freedom. This demands a boldness to act in faith — knowing full well the risk and potential personal pain which may be involved.

This section is written because the author desires that this research will be more than a polemic dialogue to be critiqued. His desire is that this study will not suffer the fate of being a mere footnote in some future study on the history of the controversy over Instrumental Music. If this study accomplishes its purpose, it will challenge both church leaders and people in the pew to throw off the shackles of human innovations and historical separation to be freed from the bondage of party division. One has nothing to lose but the shame of a broken brotherhood.

CHAPTER 12

RESTORING THE PURPOSES OF WORSHIP IN SONG

There is always the danger of becoming so wrapped up in the form of worship that the purpose and content is forgotten. Jesus often encountered this in the Pharisees. They were so intent on the traditional rules and regulations of the Sabbath day that they forgot a basic truth.

The Sabbath was made for man, and not man for the Sabbath.[1]

Jesus exposed the Pharisees as hypocrites when they criticized His disciples for not washing their hands. He quoted appropiate words from Isaiah.

THIS PEOPLE HONORS ME WITH THEIR LIPS, BUT THEIR HEART IS FAR AWAY FROM ME. BUT IN VAIN DO THEY WORSHIP ME, TEACHING AS THEIR DOCTRINES THE PRECEPTS OF MEN.[2]

Lip words without heart meaning are not acceptable worship to God. The right purposes and content of worship are as essential as the right form.

The New Testament teachings on the purposes of worshipping God in song have already been discussed.[3] There were three purposes clearly shown:

1. Express deep devotional feelings
2. Edify others
3. Praise God

This chapter will make practical applications of these New Testament teachings to the life of the church. Every generation must seek to restore the purposes of worship in song.

If these genuine purposes for worship in song are not accomplished in the body life of the church, then Christians will have a spiritual void in their lives. This void makes individuals highly susceptible to seeking after false forms of worship. If truth is not practiced, then error will arise. If genuine worship is not practiced, then counterfeits will seek to fill the void. The idolatry of the Gentiles was the end result of their neglecting to worship God when they did know Him. Paul's description of the Gentile's falling into idolatry begins with this statement:

> *For even though they knew God, they did not honor Him as God, or give thanks; but they became futile in their speculations and their foolish heart was darkened. Professing to be wise, they became fools. . .*[4]

Neglecting to worship God in the right way when it is known will lead to not knowing how to worship God. This principle is described by Paul as a reason for the deception and evil work of false teachers.

> *And for this reason God will send upon them a deluding influence so that they might believe what is false, in order that they all may be judged who did not believe the truth, but took pleasure in wickedness.*[5]

Rejecting or neglecting truth leaves a void that can easily be filled with error and wickedness. This principle perhaps explains why so much error and wickedness exists in the world.

Express Deep Feelings

One of the purposes of worship in song taught in the New Testament is to express deep personal feelings. This is evident from the context of Jesus singing with His disciples before His betrayal.[6] This is evident from the context of Paul and Silas singing in prison.[7] The clearest expression of this purpose is a statement from James.

Is anyone cheerful? Let him sing praises.[8]

If one is to restore the New Testament purposes of singing, then he must give attention to this heart-felt expression of devotional feelings.

Worship in song is *expression* of one's own deep religious feelings to God. It is not some kind of a dramatic or emotional program to *impress* the worshipper.

One can have his feelings stimulated by drugs, music, drama, dance and ceremony. Such can bring tears to the eyes, goosebumps on the arm and emotion to the voice. This is not worship. It is a physiological and psychological experience which happens within and without religious contexts. Such has nothing to do with worshipping God.

It is true that genuine worship often can stimulate these feelings. Such feelings are not the cause of true worship, nor are they to be confused with true worship. The feelings are neutral in regard to whether the worship is true or false. Pagans have similar feelings. Atheists and agnostics have similar feelings. Feelings are not to be denied, but neither are they to be made the criteria of truth.

Christian worship in song is the expression of a heart full of joy or grief. It is the expression of inward devotion of the soul. In singing one is able to purge the inner tensions of the mind and gain relief. In singing one is able, in an exalted way, to affirm his deep convictions and develop a greater boldness. In singing one is able to release the exuberant joy of his heart in thanksgiving and praise. Singing is *EXPRESSION*.

If singing is heart-felt expression, then certainly one should avoid any form of word worship. The mere enunciation of words without meaning, no matter how beautiful or pious they might be, is not worship. This would argue against "mouthing" memorized words of a song without understanding the meaning. The mere repetition of memorized phrases is not worship regardless of how long they have been a part of one's tradition. What is said must come from the heart. If God were interested in mere words, one could just play a tape containing a good song.

To illustrate the need for this teaching, let the author relate a personal experience.

As a preacher I often sit by the pulpit on a platform while the congregation is singing. It is a revealing experience.

The songs that are being sung are words of praise to the God who spoke the universe into existence and will someday bring it to consumation. It is the God who caused Sinai to quake and divided the waters of the Red Sea. He is the God before whom we stand in awe.

During the period of singing I have observed that some do not sing. They just blankly stare into nothingness. Some frivolously are passing notes or playing peek-a-boo with a baby. Some turn from side to side seeing who is present and try to give a nod of recognition if they can catch an eye. Some have their eyes set in bored silence. Some are so caught up in the harmony of the song and just enjoy participating in the blending of voices whatever the words.

How could this be? The God we praise is a great God. He desires worship from the fullness of the inward spirit. He desires the rational understanding of the mind. How could those who claim to be His worshippers be so unthoughtful and passive?

From the platform where I sit I look with disdain upon the frivolous mass of flawed worshippers.

> *Then it hits me. What am I doing? Am I not as*
> *guilty as they? Where is the inward devotion of my heart?*
> *Where is the understanding of the words I speak from rote*
> *memory? In judging others, I condemn myself.*
>
> *I see now how easy it is to fall into the error of*
> *mere word worship. I repent and renew my resolve to*
> *worship in spirit and in truth.*

Worship in song is an expression of deep personal feelings to God. Singing, whether private, in small groups or in the assembly, should have this as its purpose. When one learns to sing with this as his purpose, he will discover many things.

He will purge your heart of the superficial trash which accumulates during the process of everyday living.

He will affirm your faith anew and will be able to find the strength to become more bold in his confession of Jesus Christ.

He will have shared with others in his singing. Each voice becomes a part of the harmonious whole. He no longer feels alone. He is connected to others in the body of Christ.

He has released the bubbling joy within his heart through singing. Thanksgiving for God's benevolent care, joy because one knows the good news of Christ and peace because of his precious hope all swell up within him. He is able to let this overflowing feeling of devotion surge forth in singing.

If New Testament worship in song is to be restored in the twentieth century, then men must learn that worship is the expression of the inward devotion of the heart to God. Not only must this purpose be intellectually understood, it must also be reflected in practice.

Edify Others

A second purpose of worship in song taught in the New Testament is to edify others.[9] Worship in song involves "speaking to one another"[10] and "teaching and admonishing one another"[11]. Paul's admonition to those in the assembly at Corinth was that their singing must also edify others.

> *When you assemble, each has a psalm . . . . . Let all things be done for edification.*[12]

Singing is a vital part of maintaining the health and vitality of a congregation. It is a teaching medium; it is a motivational medium; it is a means by which unity is both expressed and maintained. It is the only way through which every member of the congregation is able to give a vocal expression of their faith at the same time.

In singing, one is able to speak deep feelings in language which would be awkward in prose. In singing, one is able to affirm deep convictions with boldness. This is partly because it is done in community and partly because it is done in poetic language.

Congregational singing is a graphic expression of unity. The different parts harmonize together to form an expression of praise more beautiful and more full than the sum total of the individual parts. There is an expression of unselfishness. One part is silent while another leads. There is an expression of dependence. Each part is needed and necessary for the completion of the whole. There is an expression of mutual concern. Admonitions flow back and forth one to another in the singing. There is an expression of togetherness as, in unison, voices are lifted in praise to God. How can those who sing together from the fullness of their hearts and the depth of their spirits ever be divided?

Singing has long been recognized for its power.[13] Songs of war have been sung to unite and motivate a people to face an enemy.[14] Songs of comfort are sung at a funeral to sooth the troubled spirits of the grieving.[15] Songs are used in protest movements to unite the thinking and convey a message.[16] Songs have the power to confirm one's faith.[17] Songs are good teaching tools.[18] *What* a congregation sings and *how* they sing will help determine the strength and vitality of the congregation. Singing is not only the expression of deep feelings of devotion, but it is also a tool of edification.

I Corinthians indicates that the church at Corinth had forgotten the edifying purpose of singing. Those who had the miraculous gift of speaking foreign languages would sing in these languages. They did not understand what they were saying. Others in the assembly could not understand what they were saying. Such songs — no matter how inspired or how beautiful — were of no value. They were not the expression of the person's heart who was uttering them, nor could they be understood by those who heard them.

Paul told them not to sing if they did not understand what they were saying or if others did not know the meaning of their words. They were ignoring the fact that one of the purposes of singing was to edify.

This same lesson needs to be understood today. A choral performance in a foreign language is not edifying. Instrumental music is not edifying. Humming, whistling or using one's voice to imitate a musical instrument is not edifying. What is sung must be understood by the mind before it can edify.

Since edifying is one of the purposes of singing, consideration should be given to the following:

Song leaders should choose songs, not because they are his favorites or because they are easily led, but because they meet the *needs* of the congregation. The need might be: to affirm faith in the time of trials; to rejoice at a time of thanksgiving; to complement teachings done from the pulpit or in Bible classes; to offer a sacrifice of praise to God. If songs are to edify, the selection of these songs should fit the need.

Songs which are sung should be according to the teachings of the Scriptures. No false teaching should be affirmed in a song, no matter how popular the song or how beautiful the harmony. Songs can be the vehicle of spreading false teaching.

Singing should be understood. Attention should be given to the words as well as the melody. The words are what carry the meaning of the message. There is no rationally understood message without them. This lesson needs to be expressed by the song leaders. This lesson should be taught in the singing schools. Singing must be understood in order to be edifying.

Singing should not be viewed as an aesthetic performace to entertain, but it must be a mutual sharing in song to build one another up in the faith. The worshipper must be the actor, not the audience, in singing; God is the audience.

It is true that others who are being edified by the teaching and admonition are also the audience. Their role is not to be passively entertained or pass judgement on the quality of the performance, but to receive instruction and motivation from those who are singing.

It is on this point that good judgment must be used in order to maintain the edifying purpose of singing. The New Testament authorizes solo singing[19] and by inference quartets and choruses.[20] Such would sometimes be very edifying. A new song composed to teach a lesson or complement a theme being emphasized in the life of the congregation could well be sung in solo or by a group. A chorus of singers often fill a special need in singing at funerals and weddings.

Opposition to choral groups and solos in the assemblies of the church has often been based upon practical reasons rather than doctrinal prohibitions.

Choral groups singing before the assembled congregation can well become, in the view of the audience, a musical performance to entertain.[21] A soloist, because of his special gift for singing, may be tempted to become proud.[22] Singing groups have a temptation to become so wrapped up in the mechanics of the music that the message is forgotten. Such practical problems have limited the use of special singing groups in the assembly of the church. If there were proper instruction and understanding about the purposes of worship in song, such practical problems could be overcome.

In private devotion, small group and congregational worship, let all things be done for edification. In teaching, preaching, praying or singing let all things be done for edification.

Praise God

A third purpose of worshipping God in song expressed in the New Testament is to praise God.[23] Christians at Ephesus and Colossae

were instructed to direct their singing to "God" or to the "Lord".[24]
The songs which were sung by Paul and Silas in prison were directed
"to God".[25] Many of the songs preserved on the Old Testament book
of Psalms are addressed to God. From both their content and their
vocabulary one learns much about praising God.

> *It is good to give thanks to the Lord, and to sing praises*
> *to Thy name, O Most High;*
>
> *O Lord, God of vengeance; God of vengeance, shine forth!*
> *Rise up, O Judge of the earth;*
>
> *O Come. let us sing for joy to the Lord; Let us shout*
> *joyfully to the rock of our salvation.*
>
> *Sing to the Lord a new song; Sing to the Lord, all the earth.*
> *Sing to the Lord, bless His name;*
>
> *O sing to the Lord a new song, for He has done wonderful*
> *things,*
>
> *Shout joyfully to the Lord, all the earth. Serve the Lord*
> *with gladness; Come before Him with joyful singing.*[26]

Jesus taught that worship, including worship in song, must be directed to God and not man. He knew that there would always be the
temptation to impress men by performing showy acts of devotion.
This motivated the Pharisees to "play to the people" rather than
"praise God". Jesus speaks thus of their error.

> *But they do all their deeds to be noticed by men; for they*
> *broaden their phylacteries, and lengthen the tassels of*
> *their garments. And they love the place of honor at*
> *banquets, and the chief seats in the synagogues, and*
> *respectful greetings in the market places, and being*
> *called by men, Rabbi.*[27]

Deeds of piety to gain the attention or praise of men do not qualify as worship to God. This applies not only to the way one dresses and to his implied status at social and religious gatherings, but also to acts of devotion themselves. Jesus plainly shows that the motivation for giving, praying and fasting is not to receive the praise of men.

> *When therefore you give alms, do not sound a trumpet before you, as the hypocrites do in the synagogues and in the streets, that they may be honored by men, Truly I say to you, they have their reward in full.*
>
> *And when you pray, you are not to be as the hypocrites; for they love to stand and pray in the synagogues and on the street corners, in order to be seen by man. Truly I say to you, they have their reward in full.*
>
> *And whenever you fast, do not put on a gloomy face as the hypocrites do; for they neglect their appearance in order to be seen fasting by men. Truly I say to you, they have their reward in full.*[28]

It is hypocrisy to pretend to praise God when in reality one is seeking to be praised by men. This was true of giving, praying and fasting in the first century, and it is true of singing in the twentieth century also.

In worshipping God one is walking on holy ground. There is a sense of awe and reverence in His presence. The profaning of the holy brings the judgement of God on man. Such was the sin of Uzzah.[29] Such was the sin of the sons of Aaron.[30]

The writer of Hebrews shows the importance of respecting the holiness of God. He describes the giving of the law on Mount Sinai with these words:

> *For you have not come to a mountain that may be touched and to a blazing fire, and to darkness and gloom and whirlwind, and to the blast of a trumpet and the sound of words which sound was such that those who heard begged that no further word should be spoken to them. For they could not bear the command, IF EVEN A BEAST TOUCHES*

> *THE MOUNTAIN, IT WILL BE STONED. And so terrible was the sight, that Moses said, I AM FULL OF FEAR AND TREMBLING.*[31]

This awesome fearful sight of coming before God on the physical Mount Sinai is then contrasted with greater awesomeness that one has in coming before God under the New Covenant.

> *But you have come to Mount Zion and to the city of the living God, the heavenly Jerusalem, and to myriads of angels, to the general assembly and church of the first-born who are enrolled in heaven, and to God the Judge of all, and to the spirits of righteous men made perfect, and to Jesus the mediator of a new covenant and to the sprinkled blood, which speaks better things than the blood of Abel.*[32]

The argument is that one should stand before God with greater fear and awe in the church than did Israel at Sinai. Standing before God either worshipping Him or receiving His word is an awesome experience. The author of Hebrews gives two exhortations based upon this great holiness of God.

> *See to it that you do not refuse Him who is speaking. For if those did not escape when they refused Him who warned them on earth, much less shall we escape who turn away from Him who warns in heaven.*
>
> *Let us show gratitude, by which we may offer to God an acceptable service*[33] *with reverence and awe; for our God is a consuming fire.*[34]

The motivation for listening to the word of God and offering acceptable sacrifice is based upon the awesome reverence one has when he comes before God. It is no thing to be taken lightly. It is no common or frivolous exercise to be regarded with disdain. God is a consuming fire!

161

The author of Hebrews gives further instruction concerning the nature and purpose of worship. He contrasts Christian worship with the sacrifices offered in Jewish worship in the temple.[35] He shows that Christian sacrifices do not consist of the blood of bulls and goats since the sacrifice of Jesus was once and for all.[36] There are sacrifices which Christians make consisting of (1) suffering, (2) fruit of lips (3) doing good.

> *Hence let us go out to Him outside the camp, bearing His*
> *reproach. . . . .Through Him then let us continually offer*
> *up a sacrifice of praise to God, that is, the fruit of lips*
> *that give thanks to His name. And do not neglect doing*
> *good and sharing; for with such sacrifices God is pleased.*[37]

The Christian sacrifices of "bearing His reproach, fruit of lips and doing good" are still being offered. The sacrifice of praise is what is involved in the "fruit of lips". The praise we give in prayer and song are sacrifices. They are to be so regarded.

God was not pleased with inferior or flawed sacrifices in the Old Testament. He sharply rebuked those who insulted the holiness of God by bringing sacrifices which were blind or lame.

> *A son honors his father, and a servant his master. Then*
> *if I am a father, where is My honor? And if I am a master,*
> *where is My respect? says the Lord of hosts to you. . . . .You*
> *are presenting defiled food upon My altar. . . . .you present*
> *the blind for sacrifice, is it not evil? . . . . . you present*
> *the lame and the sick, is it not evil? . . . . . ."You also say,*
> *My how tiresome it is! And you disdainfully sniff at it,"*
> *says the Lord of hosts, "and you bring what was taken by*
> *robbery, and what is lame or sick, so you bring the offering!*
> *Should I receive that from your hand?" says the Lord. But*
> *cursed be the swindler who has a male in his flock, and*
> *vows it, but sacrifices a blemished animal to the Lord.*[38]

Just as God refused the inferior sacrifices the Jews sought to offer at the temple, so God refuses to receive inferior sacrifices of praise to His name today. God is just as displeased with word-only singing as he was with a blind sheep or a lame goat. When our worship in song is flawed because it is done without meaning as a formal ritual, it is not an acceptable sacrifice of praise to God.

God is holy and one's worship in song should reflect this.

ENDNOTES

[1] Mark 2:27.
[2] Matthew 15:8-9 as quoted from Isaiah 29:13.
[3] See Chapter II, pages 15-20.
[4] Romans 1:21-22.
[5] II Thessalonians 2:11-12.
[6] Matthew 26:30.
[7] Acts 16:25.
[8] James 5:13.
[9] See pages 17-19.
[10] Ephesians 5:19.
[11] Colossians 3:16
[12] I Corinthians 14:26.
[13] Plato in the Republic says, "Let me make the songs of a nation and I care not who makes its laws".
[14] The "Battle Hymn of the Republic" is such a song.
[15] The song "Does Jesus Care?" is such a song.
[16] The song "We Shall Overcome" which was used in the civil rights movement is an example of this.
[17] The song "My God, He is Alive" is such a song.
[18] Many learn the books of the Bible first by singing them to a tune.
[19] I Corinthians 14:26.
[20] Nothing is said as to the number or organization of singers in the "one another singing" of Ephesians 5:19 and Colossians 3:16. Whether one, four or an hundred sing is incidental. Nothing more is being done than singing. In four part harmony one might say that there four choruses reponding to one another in song.
[21] Such is often not the desire of the singing group, but it happens because of lack of instruction and understanding on the part of the hearer.
[22] This is little different from the temptation of speakers becoming proud of their ability to speak and move people.
[23] See pages 19-20.
[24] Colossians 3:16; Ephesians 5:19.
[25] Acts 16:25.
[26] Psalms 92:1; 94:1-2; 95:1; 96:1-2; 98:1; 100:1-2.
[27] Matthew 23:5-8.

[28]Matthew 6:2, 5, 16.

[29]II Samuel 6:3-8.

[30]Leviticus 10:1-2.

[31]Hebrews 12:18-21.

[32]Hebrews 12:22-24.

[33]The word "service" is a translation of the Greek term *latreuo* . It is one of the worship words used in the New Testament. See pages 4-6.

[34]Hebrews 12:25, 28-29.

[35]A number of New Testament passages show the sacrifice motif connected with Christian worship and service. See Romans 12:1;15:16; Philippians 2:17; II Timothy 4:6; I Peter 2:5.

[36]Hebrews 7:27; 9:12, 28; 10:10.

[37]Hebrews 13:13, 15-16.

[38]Malachi 1:6-8, 13-14.

CHAPTER 13

RESTORING FELLOWSHIP TO A BROKEN BROTHERHOOD

Brotherhood in the church is not determined by man's judgment but by Divine birth. To be a child of God one must be born into God's family. This spiritual birth makes him a brother to every other child of God regardless of what his ethnic background, social standing or economic status.

> *For you are all sons of God through faith in Christ Jesus. For all of you who were baptized into Christ have clothed yourselves with Christ. There is neither slave nor free man, there is neither male nor female; for you are all one in Christ Jesus.*[1]

A person does not choose his brother on the basis of his own preference. He recognizes someone as his brother on the basis of his being a child of God. All of God's children are my brothers and sisters by rights of birth. They are God's children and that automatically makes them my family because I am His child.

There is no question that all who have been born into God's family are saved by grace.[2] There is no question about the fact that all of those in God's family are objects of special care for one another.[3] There is no question about the fact that Christians are to accept one another as Christ has accepted us.[4] This acceptance must occur even when the one to be accepted is unworthy, undesirable and full of "warts". There is no question about the fact that a Christian is not to judge his brother or regard him with contempt.[5] In fact, a Christian is instructed by Jesus to "Judge not".[6]

These are not areas of disagreement between those who seek to restore fellowship to a broken brotherhood. Members of the Conservative Christian Church and members of churches of Christ both find their historical roots in the Restoration Movement of the nineteenth century in the United States. They are presently estranged from one another in fellowship. This estrangement cannot be explained on cultural, economic and sectional grounds. It cannot be explained on the basis of power struggles between strong personalities using the tools of papers and colleges. This estrangement must be understood on theological grounds.

An Historical Perspective[7]

Major divisions within the Restoration Movement have always resulted from how men regarded the authority of the Scriptures. It is this issue that must be central in any discussion of restoring fellowship in a broken brotherhood.

The Mormon church[8], for example, broke off from the ideals of the Restoration Movement because it introduced faith and practice "which God commanded not". The Bible does not specifically condemn the Book of Mormon or the other documents which Mormons hold as inspired. The Scriptures teach their own sufficiency and that alone should be enough to exclude latter day revelations. The Mormons held to a different view of the authority and sufficiency of the Scriptures and therefore broke off from the rest of the Restoration Movement. This different view of the authority of the Scriptures influenced their practices. Their practice of divine healings, glossolalia and even polygamy came from their divergent view of Scriptural authority.

The Disciples of Christ, likewise, broke from the ideals of the Restoration Movement at the turn of the century.[9] They did so because they advocated faith and practice "which God commanded not". Before this break there existed a great variation of different judgements among brethren as they sought to come to a better knowledge of God's will revealed in the Scriptures. Fellowship could exist as long as no one demanded that "unscriptural" practices be imposed on others. The break in fellowship came because of the introduction of practices "which God commanded not" into the worship and organization of the church. Instrumental music in worship was not authorized. Missionary societies in the organization of the church were not authorized. When such were introduced into the church, then those whose faith could not tolerate them had to leave.[10]

The attitude toward Scriptural authority continued to erode until there was in many churches a complete rejection of the authority of Christ as revealed in the Scriptures. Colleges and universities supported by these churches became liberal in theology. The organization of these churches became more and more denominational. Many practices such as sprinkling infants, using women preachers and allowing denominational control were tolerated because the Scriptures are silent about them.

What had started out as a drifting away from the ideal of "Speaking where the Bible speaks and being silent where the Bible is silent" became a total rejection of the Restoration Principle by 1968. The Disciples Church completely restructured itself to become a full-fledged denomination. Since that time it has merged with other denominational groups.

A segment of the Disciples Church did not go along with the 1968 restructure. Although accepting the principle of "freedom where the Bible does not condemn", this group could not accept some of the faith and practice which was being imposed upon them in this restructuring process. The result was a broken fellowship between the conservative group and the Disciples Church. The practices of the Disciples Church, though not specifically condemned in the Scriptures, were contrary to the conservative group's own traditions and temperament. This caused them to disassociate themselves from the Disciples Church.

The result was a new fellowship identified with two names: "Instrumental Church of Christ" and "Conservative Christian Church." The first distinguishes them from churches of Christ and the latter distinguishes them from the more liberal Christian Church.

This new break between the Conservation Christian Church and the Disciples Church was similar to the break that occured in 1906. Both involved how the authority of the Scriptures was to be understood. In many ways the Conservative Christian Church today is at the same place that the Disciples Church was in 1906. The Disciples Church has carried the hermenuetical principle of "liberty where the Bible is silent" to its ultimate end. It has become evident that the seeds of a full blown digression are contained in any disregard for the prohibitive silence of the Scriptures. The Conservative Christian Church, though accepting the same hermenuetical principle, is unwilling to accept the ultimate consequences this principle allows. It finds itself on the one hand accepting the hermenuetical principles of the Disciples Church and on the other hand still holding to many of the practices found in churches of Christ.

Dialogue

Dialogue between the Conservative Christian Church and churches of Christ continues to exist. There is renewed interest in it. There is a strong desire for fellowship on both sides. Attempts are being made to understand one another. Meetings have been held to discuss the issues which divide. Much has been said about attitudes. Considerable blame has been laid at the door of "lack of communications". Grace, fellowship and brotherly love are prominent themes. All of these things are important; however, the cornerstone of the wall that divides is still how one regards the authority of the Scriptures.

Members of the churches of Christ cannot unite in fellowship with those who demand that instrumental music be maintained as a part of Christian worship. Such a practice would violate their faith and be sin. Such a practice would give acceptance to a principle of interpretation which would allow all kinds of human innovations that are not specifically condemned in the Scriptures.

Members of the Conservative Christian Church cannot unite in fellowship with those who reject instrumental music without giving up a desired practice and a long standing tradition. Such would compromise a principle of Scripture interpretation they hold — that of allowing anything that the Bible does not condemn.

Resolving Conflicts

Several things are necessary if these two conflicting philosophies are to be resolved. It is only by resolving the conflict between these philosophies that there can ever be peace in a broken brotherhood.

There must be renewed Bible study in which one brings his own faith and practice under the scrutiny of the Scriptures. The more one understands and accepts the Scriptures, the more he knows of Jesus. The closer one gets to Jesus, the closer he will be to all of God's children.

An independence must be developed which divorces the present from the traditions and/or the conflicts of the past. Human party lines must be crossed. One must not confine himself to the traditional ruts of past failures. This requires courage to stand against the pressures of brotherhood watchdogs and the wooing of compromising chameleons. This requires integrity of conviction which will speak up even when there will be those who will become a person's enemy because he tells the truth.

A consistency between faith and practice must be developed. If what is practiced is not consistent with an affirmed doctrine, let it be surrendered.

There must be a confronting of the logical consequences demanded by the principle of Bible interpretation one accepts. This must be done with honesty and humility.

There must be a desire for brotherhood based upon a real unity of faith and practice.

A Bold Proposal

Several factors are involved in erasing the estrangement which exists between the Conservative Christian Church and churches of Christ.

There can be no compromise of conviction, but there can be unselfish *agape* love.

It generally is not a conviction on the part of those in the Conservative Christian Church that one *must* use instrumental music in Christian worship to be acceptable to God. He can give it up without compromising his conviction. He can do this, even believing to himself that he does so because of his desire to yield to a weak brother. He does so, not from arrogant pride, but from *agape* love.

It is a matter of conviction on the part of one who is a member of the churches of Christ that one cannot use instrumental music in worshipping God. He cannot use it without compromising his convictions. He can exercise unselfish *agape* love to his brother who he believes is weak in faith and untaught in the Scriptures.

There can be no party spirit which seeks to minimize one's own weakness by magnifying the weakness of others. With humility and honesty there should be self examination in light of the Scriptures.

Members of churches of Christ need to look at their own failings in worshipping in song. Taking the beam out of their own eye first, they will cease from merely giving word worship in song without understanding.[11] They will seek to be consistent with what they preach about a cappella singing in the assembly by refusing to use instrumental music when singing religious songs at home or in choruses.[12] They will seek to make singing genuine heart-felt worship instead of merely an interlude between other activities of the assembly.

Members of the Conservative Christian Church need to look at their own failings in their worship. Is the use of instrumental music really authorized by the Scriptures? Does its use really help to accomplish the purposes of worship in song? Does the period that is devoted to worshipping in song become more of a performance to impress the congregation rather than letting members of the congregation express the devotion of their hearts in singing? Is it really worth having a broken fellowship with other members of the body of Christ in order to maintain a party tradition and a personal preference?

Perhaps by this means of self examination, both groups can learn better how to worship God in song. In the process they might be able to restore a broken fellowship.

There can be no fear of being labeled by either brotherhood party makers or the defenders of the status quo. Neither can there be a blatant lack of sensitivity to others within one's own tradition. One should not be guilty of berating one's own tradition to gain approval of a new tradition. Such speaks louder about one's own spiritual immaturity than it does about the roots he is rejecting.

There can be no attempt to lay the blame at the door of people who are dead. One cannot walk where they walked or be surrounded with the influences or limitations with which they had to work. One can only do what he can, with what he has, where he is. God does not judge one on whether or not he is a part of a segment of some historical movement but whether that one is serving Him in His church.

Why not go for it? Break down the wall of partition which divides. Surrender that which is not authorized in the Scriptures. Accept brothers, who in the past, have practiced that which is abhored. Learn to forgive one another with the same grace with which we seek the forgiveness of God. Learn to accept one another as Christ has accepted us with all of our weaknesses and frailties. Learn to prefer one another even when it means the sacrifice of ego. Learn to yield to one another even when it means swallowing pride. Learn to extend unqualified and undeserving love to one another even when the object of that love is unlovable. Learn to pray for one another even if it means that that the answer to the prayer demands a lot of unselfishness on the part of the one who is praying.

Would it not be a wonderful day if the Conservative Christian Church in a thousand towns announced that they are going to give up instrumental music in Christian worship because their brethren in churches of Christ cannot in good faith accept it?

Would it not be a wonderful day if members of churches of Christ in a thousand towns announce that they accept as brothers those in the Conservative Christian Church who no longer use instrumental music?[13]

Would it not be a wonderful day if members of the churches of Christ and the Conservative Christian Church would sit down together in Bible study — not to prove their own traditions but to seek to know the will of the Lord?

NOTE TO READERS:

If there are flaws in this proposal or weaknesses in dealing with the subject of this book write the author.

> *...he who practices the truth comes to the light, that his deeds may be manifested as having been wrought of God.[14]*

ENDNOTES

[1] Galatians 3:26-28.
[2] Ephesians 2:8-10.
[3] I Corinthians 12:27.
[4] Romans 15:7.
[5] Romans 14:10.
[6] Matthew 7:1.
[7] This historical perspective is written from the vantage point of one who maintains the ideals of the Restoration Movement and who is desirous of a brotherhood of all baptized believers in Jesus Christ.
[8] The Church of Jesus Christ of the Latter Day Saints, commonly known as Mormons, arose on the American frontier during the same period in which the Restoration Movement was having such great influence. Part of those within the Restoration Movement, particularly in Ohio, went into Mormonism under the leadership of Sidney Rigdon, a former Gospel preacher. The influence of the Restoration Movement on Mormonism is to be seen in the vocabulary of the Book of Mormon, some of the early leaders of Mormonism and the "steps of salvation" listed in some of their writings.
[9] 1906 is the date they were first recognized as different from churches of Christ in the US census.
[10] Those who left the Disciples Church became known as churches of Christ.
[11] Mouthing words of a spiritual song without meaning them would be no different from the

abuse of tongues in the Corinthian Christians. They were saying words in a foreign language which they did not understand. Such was no worse than saying memorized words of a spiritual song in one's own language without understanding or meaning them. See I Corinthians 14:14-16.

[12]Some would seek to justify using instrumental music outside of the assembly of the church on the basis that such is entertainment and not worship. Singing words of praise to God in a church building is no more worship than in a house or a fellowship hall. Singing words of praise to God on a performer's platform is no less worship to God than in a Christian assembly. Jesus forever showed that the place of worship was not important in his conversation with the Samaritan woman in John 4:24. What was important in worship, where ever it it done, was that it be "in spirit" and "in truth".

[13]More is involved in the division than the use of instrumental music in worship. This practice, because its use demands those who sing a cappella to either compromise their convictions or withdraw from assemblies in which instrumental music is used, seems to be the most divisive. When it is not used, the possibilities for resolving other issues would be much improved.

[14]John 3:21.

Scripture Index